SOUNDING SOLITUDE

An Approach to Transformation
in Christ by Love

SOUNDING SOLITUDE

An Approach to Transformation
in Christ by Love

Sr. Mary Paul Cutri, OCD

ICS Publications
Institute of Carmelite Studies
Washington, DC
2010

ICS Publications
2131 Lincoln Road, NE
Washington, DC 20002-1199
(800) 832-8489
www.icspublications.org

cover design Rosemary Moak, OCDS

Typeset and produced in the United States of America

Library of Congress Cataloging-in-Publication Data

Cutri, Mary Paul
  Sounding solitude: an approach to transformation in Christ by love /
by Mary Paul Cutri
    p. cm.
  ISBN 978-0-935216-81-3
  1. Spirituality—Catholic Church. 2. Solitude—Religious aspects—
Catholic Church. 3. John of the Cross, Saint, 1542–1591. 4. Teresa,
of Avila, Saint, 1515–1582 I. Title
  BX2350.65.C88 2010
  248.2'2—dc22
                                    2010008263

To all those whom God shall bring into deeper solitude,
that they may taste the fruits therein.

Abbreviations

Ascent of Mount Carmel — Asc.

Dark Night — DN

Foundations — F

Interior Castle — IC

The Book of Her Life (St. Teresa) — Life

Living Flame of Love — LF

Maxims and Counsels — M/C

Meditations on the Song of Songs — MSS

Romances — R

Spiritual Canticle — SC

Soliloquies — Sol

Way of Perfection — Way

Scripture quotes:
New Revised Standard Version, American Bible Society, New York

Quotations from:
The Collected Works of St. John of the Cross
Translation by Kieran Kavanaugh, OCD
and Otilio Rodriguez, OCD
ICS – Institute of Carmelite Studies, Washington, DC

The Collected Works of St. Teresa of Avila
Translation by Kieran Kavanaugh, OCD
and Otilio Rodriquez, OCD
ICS – Institute of Carmelite Studies, Washington, DC

Acknowledgments

My deep gratitude extends to those Nuns and Friars of the Discalced Carmelite Order who have encouraged me in the writing of this book and from whose experience I have drawn, for instruction and inspiration. To my Prioress and friend, Sr. Mary Wild, OCD, to my religious community of the Carmel of the Assumption, Latrobe, PA, and to family and friends who have supported me by prayer, interest, and love, I give heartfelt thanks, while returning my prayer and love for them. I owe deep appreciation to Fr. Marc Foley, OCD, Dr. Susan Muto, Fr. Ralph Tajak, OSB, Michael Sheridan, and Daniel Caldwell who through their helpful insights, after reading my original manuscript, have offered me suggestions, encouragement, and challenge to complete this work.

To my friends in the Secular Carmelite Community who have shared their spiritual journey with me, I express my appreciation for their openness and trust. To my spiritual director of many years, Fr. Thomas Acklin, OSB, I extend my gratitude and esteem for his offer to review this manuscript and to share his experience, comments, and suggestions with me.

Finally, to those who read this book, I pray God to inspire you between the lines and even apart from my words to seek in solitude that pearl of great price: transforming union with God in love, always deepening, never ending. To God be the honor and glory forever and ever. Amen.

Contents

Introduction

A door closes. I am alone. This is one kind of solitude.

A friend dies. I grieve terribly. This too is an experience of solitude.

I sin grievously and the heart, in tears, repents. A deeper solitude.

I love God and God is absent to my senses and mind. My heart is dry. I doubt God's love for me because I doubt my own worth. An emotional and/or psychological solitude.

I am in darkness, empty, and helpless in my journey to God, after many years of prayer and ascetical works—where is my God? What has caused this dearth? Will it ever end, this solitude of spiritual diminishment? I am inconsolable.

Solitude is not foreign to anyone. It is a universal reality which permeates all of our experiences. But why write a book about it? One answer opens the story: God. God is the One to be sought in solitude. Solitude is the milieu for contemplation, God's self-revelation to us. Solitude—which is a listening to God, a being with God, an attentiveness to God's word and wisdom, and a being-in-love with God—is worth the journey beyond the effort.

Sooner or later, if you have not found solitude, it will find you. No one escapes. Solitude for artistic, literary, or scientific purposes, although focused on these persuasions, implicitly assumes a relationship with God even when not acknowledged. God is within every solitude, unknown or unacknowledged, waiting to be discovered. God is the beauty, the truth, the goodness, the discovery to be sought.

1

Whenever we pursue these, we are seeking God. This God who draws us waits for our response. "In the inner wine cellar I drank of my Beloved. . . . There he taught me a sweet and living knowledge."[1]

New Vision

If persons enter into solitude and taste its fruits, one certain effect is that they will no longer see as they saw before, no longer behold themselves, others, or God as they did formerly. Solitude provides another way of seeing. We will be given new lenses to *in-sight*. Our eyes will have been purified by the mystery of solitude changing the heart and therefore changing the vision. The obvious is always to be discovered anew! The mystery of solitude purifies the sight, the seeing, the beholding of each person, when we are open to discovering and to receiving. When solitude brings us to God, God brings us into new vision. "Open my eyes, so that I may behold wondrous things. . . . " (Ps 119:18)

I believe more strongly as I explore the vast dimensions of solitude that there is a *comprehensiveness* about solitude, that pervades *every facet of our lives*. When we look deeply into the myriad meanings of this mysterious reality, solitude holds for us an abyss of discovery waiting to be plumbed. If this is true—and I believe it is—when we seek God, connections are made linking the whole of our lives and those of others into a communion of love and shared experience. Solitude sends us into community. One needs to enter this solitude to hear its soundings.

When God awakens in the human person the sleeping seed of desire for truth, beauty, and goodness, the mind and heart are impelled to seek God more earnestly. The yearning, weak and hidden initially, becomes a persistent ache that cannot be ignored without increasing that pain or distorting the image in which we were made. Everyone seeks completion of that latent and yet powerful craving for the fullness of love and communion inherent within us—a love and communion meant to be ultimately consummated in God.

This book is directed to all who seek God and long to know this source of beauty, truth, and goodness. It is for those who desire to "see" God and to know God's ways more truly. It is for those who are so eager to be transformed in Christ that they are willing to wade the waters of solitude. Within the "solitudes of life," we can be empowered to recognize the milieu and the revelation of divine initiative that draws persistently into the mystery of God and his ways.

Carmelite Influence

"There is no member of the Church who does not owe something to Carmel,"[2] Thomas Merton once iterated. As I attempt to explore the element of solitude in Carmelite spirituality, I am aware that every emphasis on one aspect of spirituality lends itself to overemphasis, if sight is lost of the larger picture in which every component is integrated, co-dependent, and complementary. Prayer, silence, community, work, and union with God are perceived here in *Sounding Solitude* as under the umbrella of solitude—or more aptly, within the stream of the Carmelite charism—as a pervasive and renewing quest for God. From the earliest times of Adam and Eve in the solitude of the garden, to the prophet Elijah in the solitude of Mt. Horeb, to this present day, men and women hunger for completion and for union with the living God. Within the solitudes of human life, God can disclose to us the marvelous divine mystery of which Jesus spoke: "I have come that you may have life and have it to the full" (Jn 10:10, NIV); "those who love me will keep my word and my Father will love them, and we will come to them and make our home with them." (Jn 14:23)

We are exploring a journey into God, sharing God's life and carried by God's love. This is a voyage by faith and water, by hope and blood, by love and wind. If you would enter, you will "leave a little blood behind"[3] The desire to pray, because one believes in its inestimable value and because the hunger for God pursues every person, begins the exploration to which this book invites you. Solitude is a prayer milieu: it beckons us to seek God. Prayer leads you into the solitude God wants for you. Prayer opens the door to a solitude which will, in turn, open you to God. Open the door for he knocks.

To clarify, this book explores solitude in three prime ways: as an environment for prayer, as a mystery before which I stand in awe, and as a school of faith-transformation. Within this understanding, solitude will nevermore remain only a solitude of abandonment; love is present. Nevermore will solitude remain only a solitude of emptiness; love is near. Nevermore will solitude remain only a solitude of suffering, loss, and pain; love transforms it all. Self-giving love flows from faith-transformation, "faith working through love." (Gal. 5:6)

Sounding Solitude suggests that solitude is experienced in every encounter with God. This is true simply because God is God and human beings are human beings, a substantial contrast and also an attractive one. Where God is found, some form of solitude will arise, if only the solitude of awe and reverence.

The years of prayer in solitude in the life of a contemplative religious, and for that matter, anyone who prays daily, bring an increasing desire to enter more deeply into a surrendering to God in response to being loved and being gifted. One also knows cannot do this without God's pervading grace at every moment. Solitude is not a marathon of endurance (although it may feel this way sometimes), but a total reliance upon the mercy and providence of God who calls one into solitude, into a mode of attentive listening to God's spirit of love.

Sounding Solitude is a book which assents to the reality that we are meant for communion with everyone because of our union with God, who wants this union with us more deeply than we might want it ourselves. St. John of the Cross assures us beyond countless doubts: "It should be known that if a person is seeking God, his Beloved is seeking him much more."[4]

Seeking God is already finding God. To settle, out of weariness, for an end to seeking is to sell short the transformation process that is the pilgrim's constant companion. The journey of seeking God implies an endless pursuit as one discovers the unfathomable God and the insatiable desire for God within the human heart. "Seek the Lord while he may be found." (Isa 55:6) Seeking God can be a fearsome endeavor. God alone can navigate the voyage and sustain us. It is an entry into the process of transformation in Christ by love. Its way is an endless deepening of a union with God for which we were created. It is a response in kind to God who has first loved us.

The astounding reality of those who believe and who pray is that united with God in love, the person grows in communion with everyone else and all of creation, because love includes everyone, and it alone has power to transform us and all that we touch. We begin to see all creatures *within* God as formerly we saw created reality revealing God to us. God's way of viewing creation becomes ours; God's perspective is made known to us. "I will now allure her, and bring her into the wilderness, and speak tenderly to her." (Hos 2:14)

When one is willing to risk a deeper plunging of oneself into physical solitude where one's conversation-companion is God alone, then solitude will speak its unpredicted word. This latter is an experience about which only those who know it can tell—and they probably would have little to say about it except to God and a few other close friends. The important core of each experience of solitude is to *be there with God.*

The Title

"My Beloved [is] . . .
the tranquil night
at the time of the rising dawn,
silent music,
sounding solitude,
the supper that refreshes, and deepens love."

—SC, St. 13–14

I have chosen those stanzas of *The Spiritual Canticle* of St. John of the Cross because they reveal, in delicate allegory, who the beloved is to the seeker of God.

St. John of the Cross uses the word *sounding* as an adjective to convey a solitude that "sounds" a message. *Sounding Solitude* treats of this aspect of solitude in a manner in which its soundings disclose God's ways in our life of prayer. John also acknowledges that the word can also be understood as a participle, meaning to "sound" solitude for its unfathomable depths. In this perspective, I hope to glean from some "soundings" of solitude, the echoes of the Holy Spirit's work within the human person, revealing the wealth of these unfathomable depths. The experience of solitude has endless meanings. It is a well of living water which slakes our thirst for God. Our discovery of this hidden wellspring unfolds God's presence and increases our thirst in this overwhelming process of God-search. This search becomes transformed in God's own desire to be discovered, progressively and more intimately. God's self-disclosure is given to those who seek him.

Toward a Common Understanding

Solitude requires a singleness of purpose: a person seeks solitude primarily for God. "You shall love the Lord your God, with all your heart, and with all your soul, and with all your might" (Deut 6:5). We long to return to our source.

In solitude, one remains in self-giving, so that God may "have his way" in her or his life. God wants for each of us a total transformation of the human person in Christ by love, God's love poured into the person to heal and to save, to forgive and to purify, to purge and to sanctify. All this is to bring one into union with God through likeness of love, agape. The person is being "fashioned into God" by participation—a loving intimacy.

What does one do in solitude? How does one pray when alone with God in solitude? Primarily, I acknowledge my personal misery and my absolute dependence upon God's mercy and grace for everything. "A humble, contrite heart you will not spurn." (Ps 51:17b)

Then I adore and worship; I praise and bless God.
I repent and grieve; I trust and rely upon God.
I seek and invoke; I plead and implore God to reveal himself.
I listen and heed; I welcome and wait upon God.
I desire and love; I yield and surrender to God.
I live intentionally and ardently a life of faith in, hope in,
    love for God.

All this and more I strive to do, in complete submission
to God's will in my life. Prayer in solitude allows every form
of human experience to enter our communication with the
living God.

Exploring the Terrain

To travel on common ground in our understanding of solitude
as it is explored in this book, I suggest four truths about solitude as an ambience in which we can discover deeper meanings in our personal experiences of solitude.

First, solitude is an innate experience of every human person because of who we are and who God is.

We are solitudes to ourselves;
we are solitudes to others;
we are even solitudes to God.

By reason of the gift of free will, which God will never
revoke, we can choose to sin and alienate ourselves from God.

All of us live in some form of solitude. I speak of a *solitude
of truth*, common to everyone. You are no farther from solitude
than your own heart. You cannot escape solitude's workings

in your life. You are a mystery to be discovered in gradual openings to truth.

Second, solitude and community (*koinonia*) must be in tandem, each supporting the other, each enriched by the other, each strengthened by the other, like fibers in a rope that, when increased and twisted together, form a strong cord. In solitude, one is never alone; in community, one is never without solitude. "Solitude and koinonia are not incompatible because, by one of those paradoxes of which spirituality abounds, the principle that unites persons in the most intimate koinonia is the unique, incommunicable relationship with God which each person shares with every other person."[5]

Solitude may be, at times, a negative experience by reason of our human limits, weaknesses and sinfulness or a positive experience by reason of God's lavish love and the virtues he effects in the person who seeks God in solitude. Both experiences constitute the reality of living in solitude.

Also solitude, if it is a prayerful and transforming experience, is never a solo reality. Rather, solitude is always a one-to-Another encounter, as well as a one-to-every-other encounter. Furthermore, such solitude is always, at its finest, a communion in love, a reciprocity of self-giving. *A solitude of realism and communion.*

Third, solitude, it must be admitted, emerges from its depths, as a mystery, vast as the sea, into which we plunge ever deeper so that it may disclose its riches, from light to light, from darkness to darkness. We learn gradually how to plumb the endless depths of the mystery, and we learn anew with every experience of solitude. New understanding is given with each new experience. We journey in ascending and descending spirations of new discoveries. *A solitude of progressive deepening.* A solitude whose meaning is love.

Fourth, solitude flourishes most truly in a ambience of love, a loving union with God. Only through the vision of transforming love is solitude of value. This love that creates a new creature is the call God gives to each of us.

It is God's longing for mystical marriage with each person in the fullness of eternal life, begun now and to be fulfilled in glory later. St. John of the Cross tells us: "There are many centers in God possible to the soul, each one deeper than the other, as there are degrees of love of God possible to it. A stronger love is a more unitive love. Thus we can understand why there are many mansions the Son of God declared were in His Father's house. (John 14:2)"[6]

St. John of the Cross speaks, in love's consummation, of how the Holy Spirit "elevates the soul sublimely and informs her and makes her capable of breathing in God the same spiration of love that the Father breathes in the Son and the Son in the Father, which is the Holy Spirit Himself, Who in the Father and the Son breathes out to her in this transformation, in order to unite her to Himself."[7] What an astonishing promise! *A solitude of consummate transforming love.*

In summary, in solitude we seek to experience truth, realism, and communion—a progressive deepening and broadening of our understanding of the mystery of life with God and, ultimately, a consummation in transforming love. The quest for God, burning the hearts of solitude dwellers, creates a hunger and thirst for intimacy with the living God. Solitude, in its fullness, is always a mystery of our insatiable seeking of God who seeks us more passionately and persistently than we can imagine—in fact, from all eternity into eternity.

The Four Ambiences of Solitude

Solitude of Truth

Do we want the truth? Or will we ask Jesus as Pilate did, "what is truth?" (Jn 18:38). Rhetorically, that question can be an escape from really wanting to know the painful truth; the search after truth ends by means of asking a supposedly unanswerable question. Or, it can be a projection, an attempt to provoke an answer that we can then arguably deny, as in the case of Pilate.

If the search for truth is to be authentic, the truth sought must eventually become my truth, not your truth. Morever, it must have objective value for all people in all times, as some substantial, verifiable reality: the sun rises in the east and sets in the west; God sent his Son, Jesus Christ, to save us and restore us to life with God. There are many variations on this theme of truth-searching as each of us applies the truth to his or her own mission in this world. The fuller truth becomes manifest as I discover "my truth"—or interpretation—is not "your truth." I stand alone on my ground and honor you as you stand on your ground of truth. This could be threatening if I resist your truth or enlightening; or if I welcome your aspect of the truth and let it challenge or refine mine. To be humble is to walk in the truth. The saints made this integral to their daily conversion. The solitude of truth affects everyone, especially when it pertains to self-knowledge. The light to greater growth as a person, the solitude of truth encourages each of us to live from the truth, as well as to realize one's own truth participates in everyone else's truth. What a wonderful possibility for intimate union when my solitude meets your solitude in truth!

Solitude of Realism and Communion

We are always alone and never alone! We live the mystery of our own personal call in life and we share in the mystery of each other person's mission in life. How can this be? Who can know the spirit of a person except that person themselves? Who would be so foolish as to presuppose that one's own self-knowledge tells the whole story of who he is? There needs to be an integration and a harmony between my solitude as it is known to me alone and your solitude as it reflects to me a new light about myself and a new awakening to others. A more piercing question: who would be so presumptuous to forget that God knows us more fully and truly than the combination of self-knowledge and self-reflected knowledge? God is the ultimate revealer to us of ourselves and of our relationship with others. God does this in the solitude of our hearts.

The solitude of realism incorporates all these sources of information and sees them as contributing to our welcome of a communion between us and others that participates in the triune life of God. The exploration of this type of solitude is unending. It is the story of life itself.

Solitude of Progressive Deepening

Were we comfortable with a pervasive solitude permeating our lives, we would observe the hungering need we have for going deeper and deeper into the healing haven of solitude.

But often we do not see, and therefore we do not hunger for what seems useless and empty. Solitude is not a suffocating confinement but a fresh-air expansiveness, not a binding enslavement but a profound freedom liberating us from the clutches of all kinds of bondage. As I move from a superficial, fearful approach to solitude toward a natural modality of accepting of what is common to all human beings, I can see solitude as a deep well that holds refreshing water if I am willing to plumb its depths. I progress in fathoming the inner spring of solitude little by little with each acceptance of my personal solitude and each subsequent surrender of my fears to the God who meets me where I am on the journey home. Progressively, in my quest for God, I inhale the presence and action of the Holy Spirit breathing from the core of my solitude and transforming me in love.

Solitude of Consummate Transforming Love

Our longing for consummation with the beloved carries in tow a "breathing in God the same spiration of love that the Father breaths in the Son and the Son in the Father," as mentioned earlier. How striking is the image of solitude in this immense desire of God for our complete incorporation into divine life and love! Could we ever feel more in solitude than before the mystery of the triune God wanting a consummation in love with each of us? We wait in our own secret chamber of solitude for the God who longs for spousal union with his Bride. It is the wedding of the Lamb with his spouse, the Church, and with each member of his mystical body. Transforming love reaches climax in solitude's readying of the Bride for consummate love.

The Desert

The desert, primarily the place of solitude, is a holy environment, that is, "separated" or "set apart." It cannot partake of worldly pleasures or excesses, of comfortable conveniences and luxury. It requires a setting aside or, if needed, a cutting off of what does not lead to God, the All-Holy, the completely Other. At the same time, this separation intrinsically proceeds from a universal incorporation in Christ of everyone and everything. This, in turn, leads to a more expansive communion with everyone else, but now, *from within God.* "Remove the sandals from your feet, for the place on which you are standing is holy ground" (Ex 3:5). We are called to stand on holy ground, to be united with God and with everyone and all creation, all from within God who dwells within us! Who could believe it? God reveals it.

Separation implies and presupposes commonality, or a corporate relationship from which one can separate for divine purposes. Separation never means a rift between or departure from communion with others, but rather an intensification of that union from experiencing God on holy ground, wherever that may be. In solitude, we voice a cry for the living God to manifest himself and to be the meaning for all other experiences of separation. Is it not true that lovers seek to be alone with one another? "The Beloved is not found except alone, outside and in solitude. The bride accordingly desired to find Him alone, saying, 'Who will give you to me, my brother, that I may find you alone outside and communicate to you my love.'"[8]

Alienated Separation

Where there is war, hatred, segregation, murders, terrorism, and violence of all kinds lies the most destructive form of separation. It is sin that separates harmfully. Sin is alienation, the antithesis of true solitude. Whereas sin in all its forms "tears apart," sacred solitude, as I have been speaking of it, synchronizes and integrates, giving peace, freedom, unity, communion, and true charity. One "separates," or goes apart into solitude, for the purpose of deeper communion with God and everyone else—indeed, with the whole of creation.

Where Is the Desert?

Spiritually, the desert is wherever and whenever I plunge into the mystery of God in me and I in God. Symbolically, the desert exists where God's solitude touches my solitude.

The desert is wherever one can reserve for God time, attention, prayer, and loving communication. The desert can be as close as your heart and as distant as a solitary island. The desert is less a place and more a disposition of readiness for communion with God. Our attitude toward solitude—that is, our preparation and disposition toward solitude—is the prerequisite for God to fulfill the desire he has placed in our hearts: a union in love for which we have been made. This preparation makes us congenial to dwelling within the desert of solitude. We are speaking of the attitude of tending toward God and the disposition to respond as God invites, like the attraction of a moth to the light.

Solitude, most radically, signifies "one with God." Therefore, the desert experience is a seeking of deeper union with

God. This solitude or aloneness is not isolation; rather it is all-one-ness, the truest understanding of that consistent and endless seeking after God as a response to the longing God has for us to be one with him and to live forever. Solitude can carry you into God-mystery.

God can take you into a desert of solitude when you least expect it. But most likely, God would have fortified you beforehand through suffering and endurance. God can deprive you of the desert you seek in order to give you the "desert" that is best for you—one which you would never have chosen. However it is, there will be a desert of some form of solitude sometime in your life if you have seriously ventured into prayer and self-surrender to God. In the secret chamber of one's heart or in the quiet solitude of a secluded place—wherever God finds the person desiring him and seeking him—God, who draws the person, will speak to the heart and reveal his steadfast, unconditional love.

God will call us into the wasteland of solitude where lovers meet. There, the answer to the why of having solitude is "to flee to God." Kerry Walters, in his book of the same name, calls this understanding of solitude "Soul Wilderness":

> "Soul wilderness is the place where God dwells. It's from the inner desert that God speaks to our hearts. If we would hear the divine voice, we must abide in the desert until we break through to its secret. This means embracing a desert spirituality which takes us deep into the silence and solitude of our interior landscapes."[9]

Winds That Blow

In all of our lives, there are desert winds: some, the aloneness of illness, divorce, death, or marginalization; others, winds of destitution, spiritual darkness, emptiness, and abandonment. Still other desert winds blow through our everyday living in trials, rejections, tragedies, failures, upsets, and daily responsibilities. Will we recognize the call to solitude in these circumstances? Can we see the occasions of loneliness as meeting places with God? Will the apparent "disturbances" interrupt our union with God in love? Or will our faith rise to the challenge, address God in prayer, and welcome the learning that wisdom will bring through our correspondence with the grace of the moment? Then we may begin to see everything that happens as a transformational gift of blessing. God speaks in the solitude of our hearts in every happening, no matter what it is. God's word is always a message of love. Nothing, absolutely nothing, can separate us from this love of God in Christ Jesus. (Rom 8:38–39)

Thomas Merton declared in his article "A Search For Solitude: Pursuing the Monks True Life":

"If I have needed solitude, it is because I have always so much needed the mercy of Christ and needed His humility and His Charity. How can I give love unless I have much more than I ever had?"[10]

Come into the sounding solitude and let God speak to your heart.

Chapter 1

In Silence and Hope . . .

"Ah, who has the power to heal me?
Now wholly surrender yourself!
Do not send me
any more messengers;
they cannot tell me what I must hear."

—SC, St. 6

From the earliest gospel accounts of the prelude to Jesus' public ministry to the most recent attempt of this current book, many people have written about experiences in solitude and the undeniable apostolic fruitfulness of a life of prayer in the desert.

We have heard their convictions about the experience of solidarity with all people in the midst of a life radically set apart from the physical presence of others. We know of the immense radiation of love flowing from the heart of one living so simply, so receptively, and in solitude that he or she becomes a credible voice in a world bereft of listening power. Western civilization has a tremendous need for learning the value and practice of genuinely re-creative leisure, such as the person in solitude experiences with increasing joy. In all ages, people quest for growth in self-knowledge. They feel an inherent need for time alone, and the liberating effect of living in chosen poverty. It is these persons of prayer who change the world in a positive, sanctifying way. Their apostolate of intercessory prayer, aided by solitude and simplicity of life, draws from God, for others, the light, grace, strength, and healing that is so needed today.

Furthermore, we value the courageous risk taken by women and men who have entered intense physical solitude despite the mistrust or even cynicism of a worldview that sees no meaning, other than selfishness, laziness, or mental aberration, in a life of silence and prayer in solitude—the contemplative way.

In stark contrast to the pursuers of solitude comes an adamant scream of materialism, mass-media intrigue, violence, and endless activity emanating from the abused freedom of our modern world. A truly suffocating cacophony. Within the raw chaos of postmodern fractured humanity, the human heart craves for solitude that integrates. We are a broken people longing for wholeness.

So in the light of the above, I ask the question, "why does one enter a life of solitude?" It is for this: *a faithful response to God drawing one into silence and solitude to a communion of love.* The divine lover bids his beloved to come into the solitude where God lures us. I want to speak of love and the response to love in solitude.

"The Divine Being lives in an eternal, immense solitude. He never leaves it, though concerning himself with the needs of his creatures, for he never leaves himself; and this solitude is nothing else than his divinity."[1] A French Carmelite nun, Elizabeth of the Trinity knew that from the abyss of this divine solitude, God's love flows to each of us and, thus, enables us, being filled with this love, to love in return.

To say that solitude is experienced in every encounter with God is true simply because God, the transcendent, is too much for human beings, and yet God, the immanent, chooses to dwell within human beings, a mystery of endless wonder. The years of daily prayer in solitude in the life of a contemplative religious—and for that matter, anyone who prays daily—bring an increasing desire to enter more deeply into a surrendering to God in response to being loved. One also knows one cannot do this without God's pervading grace at every moment. Solitude is not a marathon of endurance, although it may feel this way sometimes, but a total reliance upon the mercy and providence of God, who calls the person into solitude for the purpose of intimacy with God.

It is difficult to conceive of someone lavished with love who does not, at least in desire, want to return, in like love, the gift experienced. God's faithful and true abiding love remains a constant gift God offers to all of us. It is never wanting. If we accept this reality, what becomes clear is God's steadfast fidelity, no matter the response we give to his gift. God is always a loving God, always poured out in creative self-revelation, always desirous of bringing everyone home in unity and shared life.

> "She lived in solitude,
> and now in solitude has built her nest;
> And in solitude he guides her,
> he alone, who also bears
> in solitude the wound of love."
>
> —SC, St. 34

To desire to respond to that communion of life and love God proffers, one must seek the *silence* of solitude in which to listen to God's ways.

"When the soul has been established in the quietude of solitary love of her Spouse . . . she is fixed with . . . delight in God, and God in her . . . for now God is her guide and her light."[2] The silence enveloping one in solitude convicts the modern world of its meaningless noise, which pervades our days like endless waves of sound, battering our souls. To listen well, one needs to seek and to be led into a quieting of our "get-it-done" spirit, so that it can be disposed to a "let-it-be-done" spirit. We are invited by God's Holy Spirit to be still and see that God is God in whose presence we stand. "Be still, and know that I am God." (Ps 46:10)

As we explore their meaning, the words "silencing," "silenced," and "silent" draw us to a deeper understanding of how necessary and pervasive it is for persons to benefit by this gift from God: Silence. What can we glean from exploring their meaning?

Silencing

"All wound me more
and leave me dying
of, ah, I-don't-know-what behind their stammering."

—SC, St. 7

So much of our human utterance is a stammering. We grope for meaning. If a word is to be heard, I need to be silencing the noise of a restless and worried spirit. I need to be silencing the incessant inner talk of my opinions, judgments and prejudices. I need to be silencing the frenetic flow of plans, designs and projects. The gradual efforts at silencing elicit a terrifying loss. What does one do when the chattering ceases?

Is there nothing when words are muted? "All these sensory means and exercises of the faculties must, consequently, be left behind and in silence so that God Himself may effect the divine union in the soul."[3]

When faced with nothing but silence, one faces the void of oneself. We come to the self-knowledge that follows when veils and masks have dropped. St. Teresa of Jesus, who adamantly affirms the necessity of knowing oneself, says the following when describing the interior castle of the soul: "Knowing ourselves is something so important that I wouldn't want any relaxation ever in this regard however high you may have climbed into the heavens. While we are on this earth nothing is more important to us than humility. So I repeat that it is good, indeed very good, to try to enter first into the room where self-knowledge is dealt with rather than fly off to other rooms . . . In my opinion we shall never completely know ourselves if we don't strive to know God. By gazing at His grandeur, we get in touch with our own lowliness; by looking at His purity, we shall see our own filth; by pondering His humility, we shall see how far we are from being humble."[4]

This necessary silencing is the fruit of self-denial, virtue, and sacrifice. It is what we can do and must do if we seek the all-holy God. Sometimes what we do goes astray and becomes the occasion for more noise. A friend of mine once told me that he uses a mantra during prayer and discovered there were times when he used it so "frantically" that it became another noise. It got rid of the noise of distracting thoughts for a while and became another kind of noise when he felt compelled to use the mantra. It had become yet another desperate compulsion.

There is another silencing that cries to be heard. It is the silencing of the powerless by the Almighty, the eternal God's presence muting the mortal human being. It is the silencing of a human being before the immensity of God. Struck dumb before divinity."See, I am of small account; what shall I answer you? I lay my hand on my mouth." (Job 40:4)

There is a time to speak nothing. We have been taken beyond words. What is beyond asks for silence."The Father spoke one Word, which was His Son and this Word He always speaks in eternal silence, and in silence must It be heard by the soul."[5]

There comes a time when God reveals, more intimately, the divine goodness, beauty, and truth that captivates the human heart, overwhelming it and rendering it delightfully humbled. As the rays of God's love enfold the person, they leave a wound of love, aching to be healed. God silences the soul into awe.

Thus, there is a silencing that purifies, a silencing that quiets, a silencing that transforms, and a silencing that enables one to listen. It is God's work, actively preparing the person for deeper union with God in love. As the psalmist proclaims, "For God alone my soul waits in silence; from him comes my salvation." (Ps 62:1)

Having seen the necessity of silence as rich soil to foster our growth, we recognize our finitude in effecting a deeper silence that must come from God. This silence is where we would not go on our own, nor would we be able to accomplish it. We need to be silenced by Another.

Silenced

Beyond my own doing, I need to be silenced, by God and by grace, of many chatterings, even those most beautifully expressive of God's goodness and wonder. My most profound thoughts need to be humbled by the very inadequacy of human beings to know God by concepts. I need to be convinced, by grace and the gift of silence, that knowing God comes through the experience of love.

I have other "noise" that needs to be softened by silence. These are interior "shouts" of opinionated self, biased strongholds that I want to yield to no one, the rock-fast conceived certainties that hold my deluded self on pedestals of ancient standing. These pedestals must topple in the healing environs of silence. I need to be with God, standing as one before the holy, in whose presence I may be silenced by sheer transcendence. Before the All-holy, who can speak? I am silenced by the immense enthrallment of the Word. Who is like unto you, my God!

"For God alone my soul waits in silence for my hope is from him. . . . Trust in him at all times, O people."(Ps 62:5, 8)

I am mute before the ineffable. In silence I want to listen so as to hear, to hear so as to love. In silence I see a little more truly that God is God, and there is no other. The Other is One. The Other has uttered everything in love. The Other is simply to be adored.

Many years later, out of the vintage of the virtue of silence, there emerges the *prophetic* voice of silence, turned to proclamation. Out of the silence, a word bursts to be proclaimed. "Within me there is something like a burning fire shut up in my bones; I am weary with holding it in, and I cannot." (Jer 20:9)

What has been burned into one's being by silence is to be proclaimed, shared with others. The greatest proclamation is the visible living of the lessons of silence. To have learned how to love as God loves is to proclaim God. To have learned from Jesus the silence of self-surrender is to speak beyond words. What an efficacious proclamation this would be for our world today!

The God who speaks in silence is the Word that does not come back void until it has accomplished all that it had set out to do. It is the Word that becomes flesh again and again in the hearts of solitaries who steep themselves in pregnant silence. Alone and in silence, the receptive person receives the impregnating Word and, in conceiving the impregnating Word, births a new being. The person's faithfulness nurtures the whole world and all people. Life emerges. It is the generativity of contemplative prayer.

So there is a being silenced that purifies, a being silenced that quiets, a being silenced that transforms, and a being silenced that prepares one to listen.

When silencing and being silenced bear fruit, there remains a *silent person*, whom God's Word and God's Presence have stilled into receptivity. Previous to this, the person seeking God knew the *value* of silence. Now she knows, longingly and lovingly, the *experience* of silence, a lived silence. It is like the sound of exquisite music mellowing the clamor of foreign elements and bringing the soul into delicate stillness. Then the music tapers into nothing and the silence carries the melody into quiet depths . . . the still point of being. The silence of wonder.

Silent

What is heard in silence? Nothing. What is experienced in silence? Mystery. How does God speak when we seem to know nothing? How is the Word known in silence? Through contemplation. What is known? No-thing. In other words, when God is experienced, the experience is not God. What we know is *our experience* of God. But God is love. God is "known," not in concepts, not in words, not in feelings, but in love. A touch of God in one's deepest core ignites a spark and then a flame of love. The Word is silencing; the person is being silenced. A truly silent person becomes a veritable prophet. A milieu is created to make the void fertile. The prophet speaks as a mediator of God, impelled by the Word to be, in his person, a message from God to the people.

Silencing by us is active, a welcoming of the utterance of God into our inner self and, at times, evokes an experience of emptiness that needs God to fill it. We simply remain available. God is the giver.

Silencing by God is passive, the prelude to the person's communion with the ineffable who enters in silence, although hidden, where space has been made. God was not absent prior to this, but God's action was impeded. Our "noise" engulfed our capacity to receive God's word. In silence, the unheard Word purifies the intellect of distortion, delusion, projections, and rationalizations. The silent Word purges the memory of the noise of resentments, revenge, grudges, self-pity, unforgivingness—all the effects of sin. Silently, secretly, the Word frees the will from the bondage of self-interest, resistance, refusal, possessiveness, egoism, and the many roots of pride. "In silence and hope your strength lies" (Isa 30:15). If I am willing to abide in the silence, I will discover that it will carry me into a new freedom.

"Silence helps the questing spirit in us to encounter the Mystery and to experience that we are always *being held*"[6]

(Italics mine). A child knows the presence of the mother, even at a distance and, thus, is able to securely depart on his or her own pursuits, knowing she is not far. So too, the person who knows God's "holding power" as a safe enfolding is able to venture into the mystery of solitude. The capacity for authentic solitude depends upon one's trust in the holding environment each one of us experiences in our world, family, or community—and, primarily, in the loving presence of the Spirit in our lives.

Silence is also a waiting zone. How foreign to our Western enculturation which shouts: "But I have no time to wait! There are things to do. If silencing does not come to be in five minutes, I'm off to better things!" One fails to find the treasure in the field, because speed has robbed human vision of the leisure and attentiveness to look for precious discoveries. Pressed-time, impatience, and our insistence on instant "fix" have torn the silence into shreds of shattering sound. There is a time for "things to do," and there is a time for nothing but silence. It is love's sweet breathing. Let not fear of the void silence may bring rob us of its stillness and peace. Waiting until it happens excludes "making it happen." Waiting in patience and expectation will bring the lasting fruit of the gift of silence.

The Sound of Sheer Silence

Is there sound in silence? What was the gentle whisper that Elijah heard on Mt. Horeb as "finely-ground silence"? What is the sound of "sheer silence"? Most surely, this is different or, at least, slightly nuanced for each person.

The sound of silence can be described as a passive "hearing" of God's presence within oneself that quietly sends a message of divine understanding resonating through one's being like an unearned gift. The sound is a *knowing of God's ways* in a different manner than formerly. Expressed another way, the sound is *inner vision*, a seeing as never before. The sound is understood as a perceptive *assurance of being loved*. The sound generates profound peace, like stilled waters deeply plumbed. It is the silence of awe. It is "knowing God," the prototype of intimate human conjugal union. In the sound of sheer silence, God speaks the piercing Word of love, penetrating the depths of the human heart to transform it.

We come to "know" God from within the experience (a union between persons), from within the one experiencing it (each persons own spirit), and from within the experienced (God). Each is a new expression; each is another way of knowing. Why the emphasis on "knowing"? In biblical language, this knowing is intimate, spousal union toward identification with the Beloved, a transformation in the Beloved through agape. I know that I am loved; know how unconditionally I am loved; know what it is to be loved. I know love beyond understanding. I know there is a God whose love for me is incomprehensible. But that I am loved, yes, I "know."

The sound of silence, love's union, leads to our loving God, others, and ourselves more deeply and freely. There is an Italian saying, "Il silenzio è la voce di amore," meaning, "Silence is the voice of love." A Voice, speechless, and inaudible is within the silence. It is heard in the heart or in the most substantial core of one's being. We can begin to understand God's language only in the total silence of our own manner of speaking. God cannot fail to communicate God's self to one who desires God in an endless, insatiable longing. I have heard others say, "I cannot hear God; I am deaf to whatever God is saying." Or, "I cannot see God in this situation; I am blind to God's presence." How do I know God is here? Without faith, we cannot know. Without our surrender to God's Spirit in trusting love, God will not invade our freedom.

Nonetheless, as real as these experiences of presence are, they are human perceptions of a divine reality. The ineffable divine reality is held in faith and in mystery. It is known by believing and trusting the divine goodness and mercy. John of the Cross assures, "Such is faith to the soul—it informs us of matters we have never seen or known, either in themselves or in their likenesses; in fact nothing like them exists."[7]

God always wants to draw us into God's loving presence and give us a share in divine life. St. Thèrése was certain, "I know, my God, that the more you want to give us, the more you make us long for."[8] Her mentor, St. John of the Cross exclaimed: "Be still, deadening north wind; south wind come, you that waken love. . . . "[9] In the stillness, like bursts of sunshine, love is awakened.

Elijah the Prophet

What is the "sound of sheer silence" that the prophet Elijah heard, as we read in the First book of Kings, when he stood at the edge of a mountain cave as the Lord passed by? (I Kings 19:11–13) In a self-protective gesture of fear and awe before the Almighty, Elijah "wrapped his face in his mantle." What was heard was not a soundlessness; rather it was the *sound* of silence. There is, then, a sound to silence, not of sound waves touching our eardrums, but of God's noiseless touching of our hearts. After the silencing of oneself and the being silenced by

God, the person, now silent, is empowered to hear, perhaps for the first time, the *sound* of silence. God is speaking to the human heart. But this is more a listening than a hearing, more a spiritual knowing beyond explanation. It is God at the center of our being communicating divine life.

We see, in 1 Kings, that the prophet Elijah's bold and chiding comments to the four hundred and fifty prophets of Baal, "Cry aloud! . . . perhaps [your God] is asleep . . . " (I Kings 18:27) were soon to change to words of despondency and escapism—"It is enough; now, O Lord, take away my life, . . . (I Kings 19:4) following the threats of an angry and revengeful Jezebel. Elijah's success, through God's intervention, in calling down fire to consume the offering revealed a confident and yet inexperienced prophet, who himself needed to be purified through the dark night of spirit. Wastelands and deserts, mountains and meadows, and miles and miles of repetitive trust in God would release a *fire*, from within Elijah, emerging from the ashes of self-giving. The angry, zealous, murderous prophet Elijah faded, toward the end of his life, into a true man of God who knew his utter helplessness to defend himself and, therefore, his total dependence upon God to work within him.

From the solitude of truth and trust and in the sheer silence of God, there surfaced Elijah, the proven and pensive prophet, whom God would take up to glory in a chariot of fire, to be consumed in love.

We are told in the scriptures that after Elijah was strengthened by silence and the inner workings of the Spirit, God asked, "What are you doing here, Elijah?" Elijah answered, "I have been very zealous for the Lord, the God of hosts"

(I Kings 19:9–10). God said, "Return on your way to the wilderness of Damascus" (I Kings 19:15). God sent Elijah on a mission to anoint kings and a new prophet, Elisha. The silence of the one tasting solitude anticipates and prepares the person for good works, deeds fulfilling God's will and done now by the power of God. What one has heard in the silence one must speak from the silence and beyond the silence.

What does God say in the dark night? What is spoken in the silence? It is so personally intimate that no one's telling can give understanding to another. Each person passes through the silence, stays with the silence, and lets the silence speak. Silence has a message for everyone who does not attempt to escape its challenge. Like Elijah, we must let the "whispering breeze" leave its mark on us. When it does, there emerges the story of each person's transformation process, that personal and intimate story of how we come to participate in the fullness of God.

God's Thunder

Silence also *thunders* when the immensity of God, too much for human beings, is heard in the human heart. The prophet Job, who was brought to silence by God, exclaimed, "How small a whisper do we hear of him! But the thunder of his power who can understand?" (Job 26:14)

God's Word, when heard in the human heart, can resound like thunderous lightning by its sheer immensity. John of the Cross speaks of it in these words, "It's like an immense interior clamor and sound which clothes the soul in power and strength."[10]

As was the mighty wind of Pentecost, God's powerful presence, transforming the weak into prophets, creates anew, in every era, with might and miracle. God's thunder is as real as God's silence, which *stills* the person in peace by that same immensity, calming the storm. Yes, stillness also comes from the immensity of God's power. God working mightily, God working quietly — the divine omnipotence is experienced in diverse ways. Who could live with the wonder of God, if God were not to sustain us?

God's Solitude

Does God experience solitude? In *Walk With Jesus*, Henri Nouwen speaks of God's solitude on Holy Saturday in this way: "Of all the days in history, Holy Saturday — the Saturday during which the body of Jesus lay in the tomb in silence and darkness behind the large stone that was rolled against its entrance (Mark 15:46) — is *the day of God's solitude* [italics mine]. It is the day on which the whole creation waits in deep inner rest. It is the day on which no words are spoken, no proclamation made. The Word of God through whom all had been made lay buried in the darkness of the earth. Holy Saturday is the most quiet of all days. . . . This divine silence is the most fruitful silence that the world has ever known. From this silence, the Word will be spoken again to make all things new."[11] From the solitude of the tomb, divine life bursts into new day, the day of resurrection!

Holy Saturday is the day when God holds in the tomb of God's merciful love all the pain of every sinful act, all the hatred that destroys the human person, all the lack of forgiveness eating away the truth of union in community and absorbs these like a huge wave takes, in its undercurrent, the sands into the sea. God is the solitude of love. God is silent and pays every debt. What would it be like to live in God's silent solitude with such fruitfulness that it would change the world?

Dead Silence

Yet there is also a destructive silence. An antithesis to God's silence, it holds no Word in its womb. It is a ruthless refusal to be penetrated by the Word for fear of pain and suffering. It is a silence of violence. I speak of the silence of refusal, the silence of closed doors, frightened withdrawal or resentful hatred and hardened unforgivingness. As damaging as this destructive silence is to its victims, it is far more devastating, in its paralyzing effect, on the human person who inflicts it. This senseless silence thwarts the union of persons.

Dead silence plants a bold barrier of exclusion that bars any dialogue toward understanding. It is a silence that speaks piercingly: "You are not worth the trouble. There is no hope for meaningful communication with you. How could you understand? I refuse to have anything to do with you." Better called resistance to grace, a refusal to listen, the frustration of fear or obstinate unforgiveness, it is far from the precious reality of the gift of silence. Dead silence is not the fruit of love, compassion, and forgiveness. It does not reverence the other person or oneself. Quelling all efforts toward peace and reconciliation, it refuses to trust and to deny oneself the destructive pleasure of resentment and hardness of heart. Dead silence deals death. What will reverse this dead silence into paths of peace and love? Sometimes, like rare innocence amidst a plethora of destructive powers, there emerges a kind of silence, a life-giving solitude, that unites and heals because it stems from a pure love, giving trust, and mercy. This silence, in loving prayer, generates hope for effective reconciliation. The silence of self-giving love has the power to eclipse the silence of death-dealing. The story of Silenzio and Melody shows the difference between dead silence and trusting compassion when love between persons reflects God's transforming power to heal, help, and make holy.

Love in Silence

Once there was an infant boy, born mute and deaf, whose name was Silenzio. He grew to become a handsome young man having never spoken a word. Silenzio beheld all around him the beauties of nature, and these were cause for his immense joy. Silenzio observed, heard in his heart God's muted creatures, saw the trees swaying, the ocean rolling, the birds circling the skies, plants and flowers of myriad colors. He praised God for this wonderful beauty. He was happy in what he beheld. He knew God as good and gracious. Silenzio was a contented person with a quietly jubilant spirit. Although he had never heard his own voice, nor uttered a sentence, he loved everything he saw — and he saw more than eyesight could reveal. Silenzio's heart was bursting with love for God, whom he knew as giver of all good things and lover of all that he created.

One day Silenzio met a young woman, beautiful to behold, who could not see. Though blind from birth, she possessed a lovely, melodious voice. She loved to sing and regarded this gift as God's supreme blessing to her. Music visioned the harmony and wonder of all the creation that she was unable to behold with her eyes. She did not know how beautiful a woman she was, but she knew the goodness of God who had blessed her with a lovely voice to sing his praises. This she did splendidly and with great delight. Appropriately, she had been named Melody.

Melody was sitting in her garden one day, surrounded by flowerbeds of azalea, magnolia, tulips, and many other beautiful blossoms, none of which she was able to see. She imbibed their fragrance and her heart, filled with inner joy, enlarged with love. Her spirit overflowed in song. She began vocalizing the most enchanting tones of romantic love lyrics one had ever heard. Silenzio, who had been walking nearby, heard nothing. He simply beheld the beauty of this jubilant woman, whose lips moved merrily and whose bodily expression in singing was one of complete self-giving. He saw her sitting in the midst of the loveliest flowers, which enhanced the natural beauty of Melody's presence. Silenzio "heard" in his deepest heart the love outpoured, and he was set aflame. He approached Melody quietly and sat nearby, although Melody did not know this until she finished her song and sensed the presence of someone near. Startled she asked, "Who is it? I cannot see." Silenzio, not wanting to frighten her, reached to touch her hand gently. It was so assuring that it drew trust from Melody's heart. She repeated, "Who are you? Are you able to speak?" Of course, Silenzio heard nothing. But he read her lips and saw her distress and wanted her to know that he would like to speak to her although this was not possible. So he placed her hand on his forehead and nodded "no" to her question. "Oh, how sad! I am so sorry," she exclaimed. Then he touched her eyes delicately, and she understood that he too was saddened by her inability to see.

They sat together for a long time in silence, pondering the other's loss and wanting to give to the other what each possessed. The silence spoke to their hearts. They felt only love. Then Melody, touching Silenzio's eyes and then her own, spoke, "I behold beauty through your eyes. Your love frees me to see." Silenzio took her hand, placed it on her lips and then on his own, and Melody understood him to mean, "I speak and sing through your lips and voice. Your love frees me to speak." And the silence returned. Love's union broke the silence and also created a new silence. God was to be adored, whose love filled their hearts and set their spirits free to soar.

Silenzio, Melody . . . God, God, God. . . . The God of silence communicates to everyone who loves. "My Beloved [is] . . . silent music . . . sounding solitude . . . "[12]

Chapter 2

Presence and "Absence":
Felt or Believed

"Reveal Your presence,
And may the vision of Your beauty be my death;
For the sickness of love
Is not cured
Except by Your very presence and image."
—SC, St. 11

Seeking the Presence of God is the activity of human desire that longs for its completion and bliss. Felt or believed, it is the nearness of God that human desire pursues. To be with the beloved, to receive God's unconditional love, to be enveloped within the divine goodness is the longing of the person seeking God's Presence. This longing carries its own solitude: experienced at some point is the "absence" of God. It is important to distinguish between an experience of a *felt Presence* of God from an experience of a *faith Presence* of God; similarly, to distinguish between an experience of a *felt absence* of God and an experience of a *faith absence* of God. When we experience the Presence of God, felt or believed, certain recognizable consolations appear. In the beginning stages of prayer, God often consoles the person with experiences of joy, peace, exuberance, comfort. When these are later removed, the person needs to thrive on faith, believing in the God whose Presence is no longer felt.

Felt Experience of Presence

Solitude can bring light, and solitude can also bring darkness. Sometimes we see better in solitude, and sometimes we are more or less blind. In the light and darkness, the Presence of God is nuanced by the condition of the one seeking God. God seems to "look different" in the light than in the darkness. What is *felt* in the experience of God's Presence in prayer? The *effects* of God's Presence. God "touches," and we know joy or peace or love or all three. We do not know God as God, in the *felt experience* of his Presence. One could say the solitude of the *felt experience* of the Presence of God is an intimate kiss without consummation. The solitude of a *faith experience* of the Presence of God is however, union without vision. Again, in both experiences one knows an incompleteness, a missing link, which can be described as the solitude of anticipated, but not yet realized, mystical marriage. One awaits in solitude the consummation of union with God.

Another wondrous realization of the experience of God's Presence, felt or believed, occurs when one knows this Presence passively, as one who is being seen as one who is being loved, or as one who is being sustained and carried. The love can be given lavishly, as excessive as are rains flooding the boundaries of a mountain basin. This solitude is often experienced in our total helplessness to respond in like manner. We know solitude, then, as a climate of receptivity. We know solitude in the knowledge of our own poverty before divine love. Like Maria in the story of the Empty Bowl, we are in constant need of being filled.

The Empty Bowl

Maria was a young pauper girl just six years old. Daily, with a large cup in hand, she begged on the streets of her village, saying, "Please fill by bowl." She knew if she went home with a full bowl at the end of the day, she would have enough to satisfy the hunger of her younger brothers and sisters. "Please fill my bowl," she pleaded again.

Some days her bowl would be filled with cornmeal, dried beans, or lentils. Other days, she would be given rice or flour. On one cold winter day, a strong, tall man, a soldier by profession, saw Maria begging and, moved with pity, put in her bowl a gold coin worth more than the year's wages her father earned by picking grapes for a nearby landowner. But Maria, as uneducated as she was, knew not the coin's worth. She saw only that her bowl was not full.

The sky was beginning to darken toward the day's end. "Please fill by bowl," she cried. A passerby looked into the bowl and, seeing the gold piece of high value, said to Maria, "I will fill your bowl with grain if you will give me the coin in exchange." Maria was delighted, thinking, "I will go home with a full bowl." "Oh, yes, sir," she replied, "you may take the coin for the grain." Off she went, happy to have made such a good exchange unaware of the treasure she had so readily forfeited.

In our poverty and ignorance, we often exchange the priceless coin of God's *faith Presence* for the felt "fullness" of lesser worth.

Faith Experience of Presence

John of the Cross exclaims the worth of God's indwelling Presence when he says, "all your good and hope is so close to you as to be within you, or better, that you cannot be without Him."[1] Though God is within us, God's hidden Presence must be sought in concealment, in the "interior, secret chamber of the Spirit (your spirit)."[2]

When we have become trusted friends of God, upon whom he can count to be faithful even without consolations, God will give us many opportunities to prove our determination to journey with him in faith—whereby we can offer to God "a sacrifice of praise," even in the darkest moments of emptiness and pain.

The dark night becomes a constant companion that plagues us with a sense of helplessness, as though we were traveling in vain the mountain height only to see the terrain crumble beneath our feet. Questions invade our peace: Where are you, O God? What have I done to lose the awareness of your Presence? How can I retrieve it? This last question hints of a deeper reality, that of grief at loss. The truth is that we will never retrieve what God has meant to be a progression from the beginnings of prayer to a deeper faith life. Our efforts to retrieve what was sensibly consoling will end in frustration and regression. Again, "faith is the only proximate and proportionate means to union with God."[3]

It is a disheartening truth to know that I must move now in a faith that appears to be only a stark decision of fidelity in the face of hammering distractions and endless detours. Essentially this faith is the touchstone of true union with God because there is no intermediary. Faith takes us directly to God. Now faith becomes our abode in the darkest of nights.

"For by grace you have been saved through faith, and this is not your own doing; it is the gift of God—not the result of works, so that no one may boast" (Eph 2:8–9). When we believe and rely upon God as our trustworthy lover who wants only to exalt us, as John of the Cross teaches, we surrender our activity to God, who is then free to act, by his Holy Spirit, in divine ways. Faith is the modality through which our lives become increasingly more receptive to God's workings in us.

"O spring like crystal!" John of the Cross tells us, "faith is like crystal for two reasons: first, because it concerns Christ, her Spouse; second, because it has the characteristics of crystal. It is pure in its truths, and strong and clear, cleansed of errors and natural forms."[4]

The mystical doctor calls faith "a spring because from it the waters of all spiritual goods flow into the soul. Jesus Christ, in speaking with the Samaritan woman, called faith a spring, declaring that in those who believed in Him He would create a fountain whose waters would leap up into life everlasting. This water was the Spirit which believers were to receive through faith."[5]

When the darkness hides from us the awareness of God, faith tells us God is never absent; God is always immanent and active. When we seem to have no resources left and helplessness swallows our energies, faith again surfaces to enable us to trust that good will soon come. If we are confronted with "impossible" circumstances, faith gives us courage and strength to persevere in our efforts, relying upon God's grace. If our thinking is blurred by anxiety and confusion, faith supports us with its wisdom and God's provident care. We are constantly required to turn to God and to confidently expect and rely upon God's guidance and inspiration.

The challenge is great. The fruit: deeper union with God in love. The hope: complete and never-ending bliss of life with God in glory. "You know that the testing of your faith produces endurance and let endurance have its full effect, so that you may be mature and complete, lacking in nothing."(Jas 1:3–4)

Going deeper and deeper into the abyss of living in faith we plummet into the realms of mystery where no footing is to be found. We are not seeking stable ground; it cannot be found. Nor do we seek secure bastions where we can remain untroubled; that is a fantasy. Instead, as John of the Cross assures: "You should never desire satisfaction in what you understand about God, but in what you do not understand about Him."[6] Faith enables us to trust that what we do not understand can be given to us through another means, at another time. For the moment, God seems to be hidden.

Solitude's Hidden God

"You hid your face; I was dismayed."

—Ps 30:7

To live by faith is to rest on nothing less than God, unseen, unfelt, unknown by human intellect, yet a rock of refuge, the only reliable and constant lover of all persons. Out of dark faith, the dimmed ray of God-light will be the true guide through the solitude of nights, traversed in silence, "With no other light or guide than the one that burned in my heart."[7] God burns within the human heart, a fire of transforming love.

In the adventure of the spiritual journey, as one prays more and seeks to know God's ways of love, a time comes when, like a butterfly shedding its cocoon, we experience a loss of

God's Presence as the security shelter we knew until now. This experience is an initiation into a deeper sense of Presence and a new mode of relating to God: faith alone will suffice. Though we know God is omnipresent, our access to him in perceptible ways seems gone. St. John of the Cross explains, "Like a blind man he must lean on dark faith, accept it for his guide and light and rest on nothing of what he understands, tastes, feels or imagines."[8]

The pain of this transition is deep and devastating: Where are you, my God? What have I done to cause this absence? To whom do I turn, if you are not there? These and countless other questions plague the seeker of God. As John of the Cross describes, "The loving soul lives in constant suffering at the absence of her Beloved, for she is already surrendered to Him and hopes for the reward of that surrender: the surrender of the Beloved to her."[9]

Contradictions are the medium through which we can contrast the extremes so that they may be held in creative tension. The middle ground then becomes balanced and contains the truth of both poles. Absence. Presence. Absence in Presence. Presence in Absence.

The reality is that God is always present, everywhere, at all times, in everything. This is a terribly consoling realization when one is being taken through the dark night of sense and more so in the dark night of spirit. The pain comes when the person, longing to be with this "God of everywhere," discovers her own lack of readiness to welcome God, her inadequacy for the divine encounter. God is Light, and she is darkness. God is Love, and she is lovelessness. God is fullness of Life, and she is dead or dying.

The Darkness of Finitude

There is a darkness that stems from human limits: a darkness of blindness, a darkness of inadequacy, a darkness of ignorance, a darkness of weakness, a darkness of deafness to God's voice, a darkness of finiteness. In addition, our sinfulness and actual sinning leave scales on our eyes that prevent us from being aware of God. Sin and God are poles apart in very essence. There is no sin in God. When we sin grievously, we cut ourselves off from God.

> "Against you, you alone, have I sinned,
> and done what is evil in your sight,
> so that you are justified in your sentence
> and blameless when you pass judgment."
>
> —Ps 51:4

From this finitude, the person cries out in anguish, "O send out your light and your truth; let them lead me" (Ps 43:3). We know the anguish of separation from God. We know the searing pain of our human limits in seeking God. The pain can be seemingly intolerable. However, the pain stemming from our human limitations is only part of the darkness experience.

The Darkness of Infinity

There is also a darkness one encounters simply because God is conclusively too much for human beings as we are now. Yet we are made to receive God and to share God's life of loving communion. We have been gifted with a capacity and a desire to be one with the divine. God has made our nature congenial to it. Within us burns a longing for fulfillment that can only be in God, the One in whom our hearts can rest. As we yearn for the consummation of our desire for God, paradoxically, we admit "who could endure you, O God"! I long for what is too much for me, so I need to pray, "enable me, O God, to receive you. Of myself, I cannot welcome you; of myself, I cannot contain you."

In the gift of free will, we are empowered to refuse God's grace and to resist God's Holy Spirit. The quest for union with God continues, even as we recognize our capability to reject the gift when God grants it. The desire for God is greater than the possibility of refusing the gift, because the person has tasted God and has been enraptured. Fear will not keep her from seeking her beloved. "I will seek him whom my soul loves" (Song 3:2). "Come, my beloved, let us go forth into the fields. . . . There I will give you my love." (Song 7:11–12)

As we long for this union with God and also experience our personal inadequaciesand resistances to receiving God, a process of self-emptying, or self-displacement, becomes the prerequisite preamble to experiencing the inflowing of God's love in our hearts. The many other "loves" we entertain have no comparison to the love of God. They must be left behind, so that they do not prevent us from that transformation by the greater love, God, in whom all loves will come to rest. God's is a love that first transforms the self. Our welcoming of that love frees us for God to expand our capacity to receive this love. As we experience the Presence of God as absent to our unready self, God is as though God were not there. We seem so foreign to each other. How can I, who now know the miseries I bear and the many infidelities I commit, draw near to

God, the All-pure, the All-holy? "All my bones shall say, 'O Lord, who is like you?'" (Ps 35:10)

"Why are you cast down, O my soul, and why are you disquieted within me? Hope in God; for I shall again praise him, my help and my God." (Ps 43: 5)

C.S. Lewis, in his remarkably insightful way, speaks very realistically, "If we cannot 'practice the presence of God,' it is something to practice the absence of God, to become increasingly aware of our unawareness till we feel like men who should stand beside a great cataract and hear no noise, or like a man in a story who looks in a mirror and finds no face there, or a man in a dream who stretches out his hand to visible objects and gets no sensation of touch. To know that one is dreaming is to be no longer perfectly asleep."[10]

The "Absence" of God

The person experiencing God's absence knows a deep solitude evolving from the original solitude of Adam in the Garden of Eden. In creating Adam, God brought forth someone uniquely different from every other creature of God's making. Adam was alone—the first creature to know consciousness, freedom, and the ability to reason and choose. Pope John Paul II describes it thus: "Man is 'alone.' That means that he, through his own humanity, through what he is, is constituted at the same time in a unique, exclusive, unrepeatable relationship with God himself."[11]

Adam knew an immense solitude to which God responded in creating Eve. Yet even when Adam, who was given Eve "as a companion," and Eve, whose "desire was for her husband," were together, they experienced another kind of solitude, that of the difference between them, as male and female. They were companions who would need to reverence the "otherness" of each other and bow before the mystery. Then their complementarities and dependence upon each other could evolve into a new reality and personal completion.

When they were put to the test—and their desire to be like God was distorted into self-aggrandizement—they knew, after sinning, that they were naked. They stood alone and exposed before God. Each one was alone before God. The same sense of solitude which will face each of us at the moment of our passage from this earth. We will stand alone, exposed before God who comes to take us home. Solitude is the initial opening experience into life with God here on earth. Solitude is also the final experience of life as the curtain falls on our earthly existence. Solitude inherently accompanies us as human beings all of our earthly days and, as a familiar friend, it occasions us to trust its wisdom.

Truly and irrevocably, you are God and there is no other. I believe in this solitude. I trust its mystery. You, my God, omnipresent always, are still beyond me. Faith will bring me home to you, my God. This faith experience is profoundly a gift. To delight in God-being-as-no-other, is another gift from God. God wants to grant these gifts of experiential knowledge to us—ours if we but ask—according to his way and time. We are being coaxed into a somewhat unfamiliar mode of relating that will lead to a more secure and true experience of God as God is: Other.

As we enter into the vast, expanding domain of living faith, a new world of wonder captures the entire person and leads—quietly, gently, and firmly—into shared life with God that pervades the whole of one's being. The apparent absence of God is now experienced as a new Presence revealed in faith. It is the grace-full form of the Divine Dancer's movement, engaging each person in faith's solitude, so as to fill our lives and direct our actions. God is no longer a stranger in the dark night, but a lover whose place of rendezvous is faith. God is known now as the Divine Thief in the night, captor of the human heart, and constant friend and intimate. Oh, blessed faith! "Go on your way: your faith has made you well." (Lk 17:19)

Felt Experience of Absence

Inevitably, we will know the solitude of "absence" as a necessary experience, contrasting the awareness of God as he was formerly felt or believed. How does one "feel" absence? What is the *felt experience* of the absence of God? How does the *faith experience* of this same absence differ? In the light of what was previously said of the solitude intrinsic to human beings in their uniqueness, the *felt experience* of God's absence is *abandonment*. The solitude is felt, not merely as aloneness, but as abandoned aloneness. It feels as if God, who was once there for me, has left me. I am then taken to a more profound depth of solitude by the realization that what I once "possessed" is no longer my possession. The truth I learn in solitude is that God never was and never can be "my possession" in the sense of power control. Solitude brings me into stark truth where my idols shatter. I am rendered helpless to control God and, because of this, the true God is becomes able to be progressively revealed. But this is an unfamiliar God, whose Presence requires the response of my purified faith. Everything remains to be understood, it seems. I need a new mode, other than my senses and psyche, to gain the experience of God's Presence as God now wants to make it known to me.

This is why John of the Cross speaks of "a certain 'I-don't-know-what' which one feels is yet to be said, something unknown still to be spoken, and a sublime trace of God, as yet uninvestigated, revealed to the soul, a lofty understanding of God which cannot be put into words. Hence, she calls this something 'I don't-know-what.' If what I understand wounds me with love, this which I do not understand completely, yet have sublime experience of, is death to me."[12]

Enter: the *faith experience* of the absent Presence. Formerly I believed in the ubiquitous God from whose Presence I could not hide. "Where can I go from your spirit? Or where can I flee from your presence?" (Ps 139:7)

Now I am faced with the God who is always hidden, always yet to be known. God has brought me in prayer to the edge of frustration. God is manifesting "I am a hidden God. You cannot see my face." Yet my whole being cries out, "Where have you hidden, beloved? I want to see your face. I sought you and you were gone."

In our longing for God, we are to pray and to ask for the gift of a living faith, of ardent love, the grace of the desire for God, which is the pledge and promise of all that is to follow. As Meister Eckhart phrased it, "Seek God, so as never to find Him." The seeking is the effect of the desire for God. It must never stop. St. Catherine of Sienna, in her *Dialogue on Divine Providence*, expresses this with impassioned beauty: "Eternal God, eternal Trinity. . . . You are a mystery as deep as the sea; the more I search, the more I find, and the more I find the more

I search for you. But I can never be satisfied; what I received will ever leave me desiring more. "[13]

John of the Cross describes the process of transformation by love in regard to the experience of absence: "Through this love she departed from all creatures and from herself, and yet she must suffer her Beloved's absence for she is not freed from mortal flesh as enjoyment of Him in glory of eternity requires."[14]

Faith Experience of Absence

"Now faith is the assurance of things hoped for,
the conviction of things not seen."

—Hebrews 11:1

Solitude's *faith experience* of the so-called absence of God is one of *transcendence.* "You are God and there is no other." Your complete otherness, disclosed in solitude, draws my faith beyond its infancy stage. I must either transcend to where you are or be without you, or so it seems. The "where you are" is in your utter, absolute, and unattainable *transcendence.* "If a person should desire to see, he would be in darkness as regards God more quickly than if he opened his eyes to the blinding brightness of the sun."[15] "He must pass beyond everything to unknowing."[16]

When I am willing to know God as beyond all else, I am invited into a world of faith. This realization calls for adoration. Then God will initiate and deepen my quest for divine intimacy, which includes the pain of unfamiliar paths, the suffering of loss and false security, the demise of all that I relied upon to take me to God. "The loving soul lives in constant suffering at the absence of the Beloved, for she is already surrendered to Him and hopes for the reward of that surrender: the surrender of the Beloved to her."[17]

No one knows how long this absence of God will be experienced. For many, it can be a constant companion, perhaps spanning many years. However, this *faith experience*, precisely because it is a deepening of faith, leaves the person more assured of the reliability of faith to bring her to God. The person is now "Supported by faith alone, which is the only proximate and proportionate means to union with God."[18] As St. Paul revealed, it is "the word of God, which is now at work in you who believe." (I Thess. 2:13)

This supposed absence is now known as a Presence in a new way: one of believing in it, no matter what is felt. The person has been brought to a maturing faith which cannot rely upon feelings to survive. It has its own sustenance, God.

CHAPTER 3

Solitude's Idols and Demons

If we remain in solitude for some length of time, solitude instructs us and enlightens the dark crevices of our self-protection to bring us to deeper self-knowledge, whether or not we like to look at it. In solitude, facing the truth about ourselves is a desert flower we cannot ignore. In another image, this two-edged sword has a way of incising our most favorite illusions and shattering the fond images of ourselves that we would be ashamed to admit we adore.

St. Teresa of Jesus wrote: "So I repeat that it is good, indeed very good, to try to enter first into the room where self-knowledge is dealt with rather than fly off to other rooms. This is the right road, and if we can journey along a safe and level path, why should we want wings to fly? Rather, let's strive to make more progress in self-knowledge. In my opinion we shall never completely know ourselves if we don't strive to know God."[1]

The first opening to this self-knowledge comes with the enlightenment that illusions are really illusions. We would deny this vehemently. St. John of the Cross tells us: "All the soul's infirmities are brought to light; they are set before its eyes to be felt and healed."[2]

A later enlightenment brings the awareness that perhaps these illusions have power over us. "Not over me! I am determined not to be influenced. I'm in control." Still another growing awareness is that these powerful illusions must be shattered if I am to move from idol-worship to the true God. "Give up the familiar? Part with my way of doing it? Nonsense!" Solitude can be the place where we hew idols, if we rely upon our own gifts, or solitude can be the iconoclast, which will tolerate no other god but the living God.

In the early stages, when one enters solitude the person's ignorance, inexperience and emotional needs leave one vulnerable to illusion, especially if a high idealism has wrapped the person in garments of many colors of anticipated expectations. We are brought into a spiritual reality check.

We seek God and find ourselves. We ask for the light of God, and our own inner world of motives and interests are illuminated as selfish. We want to love God freely, and the bondage to our attachments, even to holy things and to God-as-we-fashion-God, deprives us of what we seek. We long to pray and be with God, and the thousand voices of me, mine, and myself thunder through the corridors of solitude. It is a kairos moment waiting to break through an ancient and familiar time zone of our own making. Our degree of resistance determines the length of this process of liberation. God shows us ourselves that we might, in turn, show God our need and then cry for help. "If goodness lead him not, yet weariness may toss him to my breast," says George Herbert in his poem, *The Pulley*.[3] "Out of the depths I cry to You, O Lord." (Ps 130:1)

In mercy, God unmasks our idols to reveal the false gods we have worshipped for years, to our unknowing or denial. This light is an immense blessing toward real union with the real God. With limited self-knowledge and our human inclination to underestimate the potential God gives us—or perhaps simply fearful and unwilling to use this potential—we often prefer to settle for a god of our own making: stoic, remote, unapproachable or, at least, manageable. Or if we view God as a fearsome judge, we tend to distance ourselves from a God whom we perceive as demanding, condemning, and punishing. Even when we can acknowledge such truths, we easily deny their operation within us. Idols are tenacious and often unrecognized as such.

Before what or whom do I burn incense? Who claims my homage? In the free space of solitude, my hypocrisy is exposed. The waters of truth wash away the numerous idols I have enthroned in error. Solitude, by its very exposure, purifies and dismisses the fallacies of worship. Only One must be adored: God. Possessions, persons, self—all idols of my making must recede before the wonder of God, revealed in faith to the deep solitude of the human heart.

The most tenacious idol to fall is the worship of our own ego. How magnificently we have toiled to establish our identity! How can this topple if I am to be a "someone" who can serve God? The rationalizations abound! The ego is not to be annihilated; it has served us well. It is to be transformed. How can God annihilate the ego when God created the human being and pronounced it good? However, the ego's submission to God as center becomes its transcendence beyond its own limits. Although the ego experiences the supplanting of its center-stage position as diminishment, will, when redeemed, participate, in a more true way, as servant to the King, God.

The "I," which in younger years sought its identity in order to have something to give, now, with hard-earned wisdom and the grace of God, lays its identity at the feet of its lover, Christ Jesus, to become with him a sacrifice of praise to the living God. "I" has become "we" and "we" becomes eventually "you, my God," a transformation by faith, hope, and love. When this happens, the primordial beauty of the human person, seeping through layers of finitude, pain, suffering, diminishment, and transformation, effuses the new fragrance of Christ. The ego, the self, the whole person, now integrated with Christ in God's life, are thus transformed. I no longer live, but Christ lives in me. "As you therefore have received Christ Jesus the Lord, continue to live your lives in him . . . for in him the whole fullness of deity dwells bodily, and you have come to fullness in him." (Col 2:6, 9–10)

Transformation of Consciousness

As idols shatter and we are given new sight, through the vision of Jesus and his teachings, our God is, so to speak, "remade" in our minds each time we receive a new enlightenment. This transformation of consciousness moves us toward a greater and deeper penetration into the beauty, truth, and good which is the true God. This discovery will never end. God is ever to be discovered anew.

Though the process of transformation is a long one, solitude has become a milieu for the person to make room for the true and living God to come forth. Transpiring is a purification of heart and mind, which will open to new freedom in a liberated person's new heart and new spirit. This liberation, as a fruit of solitude, is like a sunburst of radiance from the tomb of the risen Christ. We are virtually glorying in the resurrection. The story of Luke's account of the disciples walking with Jesus on the road to Emmaus conveys this meaning: "Were not our hearts burning within us, while he was talking to us on the road, while he was opening the scriptures to us?" (Lk 24:32) They saw in Jesus Christ the true God. They saw him in a new way. It was a gradual discovery. Jesus opened new vistas to them, in their solitude, as their own hearts were purified of hopelessness, leaving portals of new freedom, no long shuttered to the truth.

Recall, as they were talking and discussing, Jesus came near and went with them, but their eyes were kept from recognizing him. The disciples were prevented from seeing Jesus as the Jesus they knew. This was the risen Lord who was to be recognized. New eyes for new vision. Out of the solitude of their blindness emerged a new awakening.

The disciples saw suffering and death as final and destructive of their hopes. "We had hoped that he was the one to redeem Israel." Remember this occurred after Jesus' resurrection. The disciples knew the women had seen an angel, an empty tomb, but not the body of Jesus. "Oh, how foolish you are and how slow of heart to believe all that the prophets have declared!" Jesus told them chidingly. (Lk 24:25)

Jesus would shatter their idols of a messiah who could not suffer and could not die. Incomprehensible to human logic! However, it is entirely true of the God who so loved us as to give us his Son for our redemption and glorification, in a sacrifice more complete than that of Isaac.

Throughout the gospel narratives, we discover the human resistance to the value of suffering and to its purpose in the designs of salvation history. Peter, scandalized, insists, when Jesus declared he must go to Jerusalem and undergo great suffering, be killed and on the third day be raised: " 'God forbid it, Lord! This must never happen to you' " (Mt 16:22). Again when Jesus comes to wash his feet as a gesture of union with him, Peter protests, "You will never wash my feet." (Jn 13:8)

In our human understanding, pain, suffering, the cross, and similar unwanted experiences are to be shunned, denied, or rejected—avoided at all costs. In the realm of faith, these experiences are at the heart of the Paschal mystery of Jesus Christ into which we are called to enter and participate. " 'Unless I wash you, you have no share with me.' Simon Peter said to him, 'Lord, not my feet only but also my hands and my head!' " (Jn 13:9)

Here, in the shattering of idols, we see, more vividly, another form of living the mystery of solitude, the solitude of paradoxes, in which are immersed all the mysteries of gospel living. In the wonderful reversals that take place in the conversion of sinners and in the enigmatic work of our salvation, hearts are turned from the worship of falsehood to the surrender to the truth, Jesus Christ, source of Life.

As our lives know many "shatterings" of false idols, so in the depth of our emptiness God reveals himself. As idols go, the true and living God, who has been concealed by our own opaqueness and resistance, shines forth to our new vision. Releasing the familiar, we are free for new intimacy. As did they, we plead, " 'stay with us, because it is almost evening and the day is now nearly over.' So he went in to stay with them. When he was at table with them, he took bread, blessed and broke it, and gave it to them. Then their eyes were opened, and they recognized him; and he vanished from their sight" (Lk 24:29–31). The breaking of bread each day in the Eucharistic celebration is God's astounding gift, Jesus, nourishing the hungry hearts of all whose eyes have been opened and who now seek to be one with the living God.

Demons

Roaming demons have an uncanny attraction to desert places. Is it because the desert is so vast? Or desolate? Or, simply, because someone has gone there to pray? More so, demons like to return to the houses left unkempt, without sweeping. Filled with a few cobwebs, swept houses are sometimes even more inviting!

Why are we so prey to the influence of demons? Perhaps because we are easily deceived by lies. Perhaps because we like to play with enticements. Perhaps because our self-pleasures overwhelm us. Most surely, however, our succumbing to temptations stems from some measure of self-aggrandizement, sinful self-will, and a large dose of self-illusion that thrives on being "like God."

We have our unique blindspots, none so blind, however, as when we say we see. Solitude as a prayer environment will eventually occasion the awareness of our weakest link. The weakest link is the site of vulnerability through which the evil one's powers will pierce. The weakest link is unique to each person.

Taking refuge in solitude where one's weakest link is gradually disclosed is modeled on Jesus' own experience: prayer and fasting.The person in solitude is chastened to humility through humiliation, to self-forgetfulness through the necessity of sheer trust in God, to purity of heart through temptation and inner conversion, to fidelity through steadfast perseverance. There is no escaping the process; it cannot be bypassed. One enters solitude knowing that transformation in love will be accomplished as God finds a dwelling place in the hearts of those who are poor in spirit.

Inner Demons

Perhaps some of these prominent demons emerge from within our own personality structures: our tendency to rationalize; our patterns of compromise; our distorted judgments; our denials of unwanted tendencies in ourselves; our self-delusions; our unredeemed piety; and many more proclivities, uniquely personalized, to which we cling with tenacity. In solitude, facing one's dark side means facing the demons within, which we have never confronted or perhaps even recognized, never wanting to know for fear of needing to change. Most likely though, this dark side has given us hints of self-destruction that we have suppressed or deferred from exposing because never was there time to deal with them. Solitude gives us the time and the place without any further excuses accepted.

No avoidance technique will exclude us from facing these hindrances, simply because they are hindrances to what one in solitude desires most: that union with God in love, which requires a transformation process.

There is no denying the process occurs in everyday life situations and in all our relationships with other persons. Every person of faith, who seeks to heed seriously the gospel message and to develop a life of prayer and service to others, meets many demons on the way. Life in solitude has no monopoly. However, if one has decided to spend some extended time in solitude, one has, by that choice, opted for some conversion of sorts that has seemed necessary to one's spiritual growth. The choice to remain with the Lord in prayer and, especially, in listening means a commitment to change when light is given, to turn again and again to Jesus as the one mediator and model in our movement toward the Father and his will. We are to be willing to part with all that prevents our direct attention and fidelity to the Lord.

Fathers of Lies

If a person is determined to live the gospel, demons will arise to disturb, divert, mock, discourage, deceive, or tempt. "You will not die, if you eat the fruit. You will become like God, knowing good and evil!" Such intrigues by Satan play, masterfully, into the human desire "to be God." What irony that being like God, to which we are truly called, should be distorted to the level of human knowledge! The appeal is to match God in "knowing." Rather, our true "being like God" is in loving obedience to the wisdom of God's will as we participate in God's life, rather than avidly lusting for God's power as our own. Lies abound with satanic temptations.

Perhaps a more subtle taunt would be more apt today. "You do not have to forego the pleasures of the world. All things are good. God made them for your enjoyment. Be a free spirit and choose life (meaning pleasure and power)." Evil powers entice us to avoid self-giving love, agape.

Still another more oblique temptation is: "God can be found anywhere. Let your service to others be your prayer. Jesus asked us to love one another. What more need be done? The hardest way is not the best way. Must you choose to go apart from others to find God? Do you consider yourself more advanced than others? Or are you simply avoiding the difficulties of establishing relationships with others?" Ah, these really touch the heart of the spiritual life! Each of these statements and questions hold an important truth. The demons know that and so do we, to some extent. But recall that Jesus said Satan is a liar and the father of lies. In each of these questionings is also a lie, a distortion of the truth, an absence of the total reality. We want to look at each of these queries.

We are created in the image and likeness of God. Are we not meant to be gods—or a little less?

"Yet you have made him little less than a god;
with glory and honor you crowned him,
gave him power over the works of your hands,
put all things under his feet."

—Ps 8:11–1

The fallacy is to think that likeness means equality. The lie is "you are no longer dependent upon God." That lie is unmasked and denounced to the person living in solitude. That person knows, with "burned in" truth, that without God one can do nothing. "Those who abide in me and I in them bear much fruit, because apart from me you can do nothing." (Jn 15:5)

Everything from God's hand is good—true. God made the beauties of earth that we human beings may use them and enjoy them. The lie is the false assumption that all good things from God are used well by human beings. Enjoyment of good things for selfish reasons is to disdain the gift. The person living in solitude, actually experiencing her or his own poverty and complete dependence upon God, learns to respect all of creation and to reverence its gift through care and proper use. "The heavens proclaim the glory of God and the firmament shows forth the work of his hands." (Ps 19:1)

Surely charity toward our neighbor holds prime after our love for God, but God holds the primacy and alone is worthy of our foremost attention. "You shall love the Lord your God with all your heart and with all your soul and with all your might." (Deut 6:4)

The lie behind charitable service rests in the strong emphasis upon our doing of deeds—or works without faith—rather than our being with God; our works for God—rather than our love of God. Love of God's gifts, rather than love of the giver. The inversion of priorities begets the lie, not the deed-doing. All our possible good works come from the love God gives us and that we are to give to one another. It is easy to engage in works of love for our own attention and praise. It is rare to do deeds, unseen and without acclaim, for the pure motive of love of God. Were there no one else on this earth but ourselves, we would fulfill all justice by loving, worshipping, and surrendering to God, if that could be done with the purest of motives—God alone granting this.

In our union with God in solitude, our lies, like serpent skins shed, occasion the new vision of being freed through inner transformation. Lies are the demons that are cast out by truth and love. A sad finale to a self-destructive lie is found in the fifth chapter of the Acts of the Apostles 1–11. It is the story of the lie that tripped itself.

"But a man named Ananias, with the consent of his wife Sapphira sold a piece of property; with his wife's knowledge, he kept back some of the proceeds, and brought only a part and laid it at the apostles' feet. 'Ananias,' Peter asked, 'why has Satan filled your heart to lie to the Holy Spirit and to keep back part of the proceeds of the land? While it remained unsold, did it not remain your own? And after it was sold, were not the proceeds at your disposal? How is it that you have contrived this deed in your heart? You did not lie to us, but to God!' Now when Ananias heard these words, he fell down and died. And great fear seized all who heard of it. The young men came and wrapped up his body, then carried him out and buried him. After an interval of about three hours his wife came in, not knowing what had happened. Peter said to her, 'Tell me whether you and your husband sold the land for such and such a price.' And she said, 'Yes, that was the price.' Then Peter said to her, 'How is it that you have agreed together to put the Spirit of the Lord to the test? Look, the feet of those who have buried your husband are at the door, and they will carry you out.' Immediately she fell down at his feet and died. When the young men came in they found her dead, so they carried her out and buried her beside her husband. And great fear seized the whole church and all who heard of these things."

The lie was contrived in the heart. "Why has Satan filled your heart?" as Peter had asked. It was a lie to the Holy Spirit, God, who knows our hearts. Ananias and Sapphira put the Spirit to the test and deceived themselves. No one had compelled them to give the money or even a set amount of the money. Our lies fall on our own head. They are the temptations of the "desire of the flesh, the desire of the eyes, the pride in riches" as John the Evangelist tells us. (I Jn 2:16)

In her work, *Finite and Eternal Being*, Edith Stein wrote,

"For the lie is not, like an error, a failure to recognize the truth or putative knowledge but rather *an attempt to destroy the truth*, an abortive attempt since truth shatters every lie."[4]

Satan is a deceiver from the beginning, whereas God cannot deceive because God is the Truth. In solitude, one parts with idols by the sheer perception of the true God. The light of truth dispels the lies, if we choose to see and God enables us."Salvation, glory and power to our God: his judgments are honest and true." (Rev 19:1–2)

In solitude, after many shattering of idols and denouncing of demons, we come to experience the beginnings—and then progress—of a growing intimacy with the true and living God, who reveals the truth to us in Jesus Christ. We know that even if we deny God, God will be true because God cannot betray himself. "If we are faithless, he remains faithful, for he cannot deny himself." (II Tim 2:13)

Through a process of continuous and complete surrender to God and a renouncement of Satan's intrigues, the person, faithful in solitude and prayer, is increasingly released into inner freedom, which the father of lies despises, being unable any longer to lure the solitary into realms of darkness. We are children of light and called to live in that light of Christ.

Chapter 4

Solitude's Intimacy

To be alone with God, day after day, in solitude is like a deep flowing river whose tides change through shifting positions of sun and moon, wind and rain, while the movement and beauty remain constant. God is always to be discovered, always manifesting more of God's ways to us. As constant as the flow of love and splendid beauty is from God to all creation, God seeks, to our astonishment, a progressive intimacy with each human being. To believe this truth, that we are intensely and individually loved by God, is to be freed for that very intimacy to happen. Faith brings us into God.

Each of us has with God a relationship of many faces. We have moods and seasons, high and low tides, deeper and lighter times of grace, all common to a growing intimacy. If friendship is to develop, and more so with spousal intimacy, the two involved need to commit to each other time, communication, respect for personal boundaries, and implicit trust in the other's fidelity. Long times in solitude and prayer make those commitments possible and plausible. God waits for us to come into the awareness of his presence, to be awakened to God's love, to spend time in listening to God and abiding in God. Some of us have done this many times; for some persons, many years. Each time with God in prayer is new. We grow and are different when coming to God again and again in prayer. Ah, you may contend, "but it seems to me the same; no different day after day." And I reply, "always new, always different, even in so-called emptiness and regression!" I say this on the word of God, "Come to me, all you who thirst and I will refresh you." "Faith is the substance of things to be hoped for." (Rom 8:9)

St. Teresa of Jesus was convinced when she said, "Failure to communicate with a person causes both estrangement and a failure to know how to speak with him."[1] She cautions us never to give up prayer, never. Teresa forewarns us, after she had been tempted by Satan to cease praying because her laxity at the time evoked feelings of being unworthy to approach God, "To give up prayer was the greatest evil. . . . I don't think losing the way means anything else than giving up prayer."[2] How eager God is to enliven us and to set our hearts on "living fire"! Will we fear the flames of love? Or walk into their purifying place of peace? Solitude is calling us.

Theological Virtues

It is a *faith life* we are to live more deeply each time we pray. Faith brings us directly to God and is itself a real intimacy.

It is a *hope life* we are called to live more deeply each time we pray. Hope brings us directly to God and is itself another form of intimacy.

It is a *love life* we are called to live more deeply each time we pray. Love brings us directly to God and is itself the climax and substance of intimacy. "These acts of love are most precious; one of them is more meritorious and valuable than all the deeds a person may have performed in his whole life without this transformation—however, great they may have been."[3] "Love bears all things, believes all things, hopes all things, endures all things." (I Cor 13:7)

If I am centered in these theological virtues that take me directly to God, I am fed at the source. I believe God is light in the darkness. Although I do not see God, God's light guides me in secret. I believe God is there when the absence terrifies me. Although I do not feel God, God strengthens me. I believe God continues to love me when I doubt my self-worth. Although I do not know the warmth of love, God is love within me. I believe I am called to holiness of life even when my sins remove my innocence. While I stumble toward a new conversion, God is merciful and forgiving.

I believe God does not abandon me when all hell breaks loose in temptation's hour. Although I cannot grasp God's hand, God is my shield and defense.

I believe God is trustworthy when all else fails. Even as the loss diminishes me, God is faithful and steadfast.

This active faith becomes the food of my life and soothing water, as I thirst in the desert of solitude. This living and persevering faith is what makes the saints. It is what has carried Christians and the church through centuries of gospel living and persecution. I have heard it described that the difference between tradition and the traditional is that tradition is the living faith of dead people, and the traditional is the dead faith of living people. The former brings us into union with the living God who gives us life by raising the "dead."

Along with the virtues of hope and charity, the theological powers God has given us at baptism become the radical substance of a life of prayer in solitude and a life of service in community. A person can thrive on these when everything else is relinquished or taken away.

These *virtues to God*, as theological, if lived to the hilt, will bring the human person to share the very life of the Trinity. By the indwelling Spirit, we welcome, receive, and are transformed in the Father's self-giving to the Son and the Son's self-giving to the Father, so that we move, breathe, and act by the same Spirit of love. "You will know that I am in my Father, and you in me, and I in you. . . . those who love me will be loved by my Father, and I will love them and reveal myself to them." (Jn 14:20, 21)

Vintage Wine

Does intimacy ever feel "non-intimate"? Most surely, if it is real. God knows we could not bear a continuous touch of divinity! Union in love, as in marriage when couples have lived with each other for fifty or sixty years, truly grows deeper, mostly unknown to the couple, and is certainly indescribable. Swift white wings of sacrifice, endurance, self-giving, and repeated forgiveness have whisked away the seeds of mistrust, jealousy, competitiveness, and power lust that so often germinate into wild weeds, excluding intimacy.

Years of "knowing" each other have left their indelible mark, enlightening each one in the truth that what is known of the other is extremely little compared to what is yet to be discovered. They understand that what is known is known through love shared, roots growing silently and hidden in the cool earth, to support the supra-structure of a gigantic live oak, which spreads broad and high in love's expansion. It is the flow of aged love; it is vintage now grown pure and refined like wine. It is the voiceless expression of nearness and abiding presence.

So it is with God and the person in solitude. God, who first loves us and who has seeped through our resistances for many years, now enables us to accept and believe in that steadfast, unconditional love of God. Little by little we have learned to love as God loves and with God's own spiritual love. Words have lapsed into shared life and trusting surrender. There is no need to know anything more, but just to be in each other's presence, savoring the beauty of simple things and delighting in all that is. God will work the transformation in our deepest core, gradually, quietly, surely."My Beloved is mine and I am his." (Song 2:16)

The unknown is to be reverenced with awe and thanksgiving. Silent solitude nurtures the esteem for mystery. In our surrender to the Other, we breathe in the Spirit of God, who is our lone intimate. This intimacy is of "the Lover with His beloved, transforming the beloved in her Lover."[4]

"I abandoned and forgot myself,
Laying my face on my Beloved;
All things ceased; I went out from myself,
Leaving my cares forgotten among the lilies."[5]

John of the Cross knew the wonder of Christ's unfathomable mystery: "There is so much to fathom in Christ, for He is like an abundant mine with many recesses of treasures, so that however deep men go, they never reach that end or bottom, but rather in every recess find new veins with new riches everywhere."[6]

During our times of prayer, transpiring in solitude is a union within a communion: a foursome of persons, the Father,

Son, Holy Spirit, and the pray-er. If I pray to one of the Divine Persons, the others humbly defer to this one Person, while all know what is going on and are always present. What magnificence! It is even better than I can explain. Intimacy in solitude is an abandonment to God's loving embrace. Oh, holy solitude that brings such refreshing repose!

"How gently and lovingly, You awake in my heart,
Where in secret You dwell alone;
And by Your sweet breathing, filled with good and glory,
How tenderly You swell my heart with love."[7]

Intimacy of the Indwelling Spirit

"If you love me, you will keep my commandments. And I will ask the Father, and he will give you another Advocate, to be with you forever. This is the Spirit of truth, whom the world cannot receive, because it neither sees him nor knows him. You know him, because he abides with you, and he will be in you." (Jn 14:15–17)

This astonishing passage of sacred scripture brings joy into the hearts of those who believe, a joy that no one can take from us. Jesus wanted this joy to remain with us so intimately that, in addition to the Eucharistic presence, his Spirit dwells within us. We are temples of the living God!

To ponder this reality of faith is redolent of the incarnation mystery, announced to Mary, wherein the Word became flesh. It is redolent also of Jesus' words: "we will come to you and make our home in you." How intimate the announcement that we become God's home. It would be unbelievable had not God uttered the words.

Imagine the graced intimacy of that enforced solitude — the prisoner, the widow, the abandoned child, the rejected invalid — when those who are lonely meet the indwelling Holy Spirit who speaks, "I am with you and I love you. You are precious in my sight." We are asked to abide in this divine love; we are invited to remain with the indwelling presence of God and receive this perfect acceptance of who we are now. God will never depart unless we choose it by sin. This spousal intimacy is graced life. God wants it for each of us. The solitude of loneliness then evolves into the solitude of intimacy when the Holy Spirit enkindles in us the fire of his divine love. Solitude is a celebration of this mystery of divine indwelling.

Elizabeth of the Trinity, a nineteenth-century French Carmelite, rejoiced to discover: "We carry our heaven within us, since he who completely satisfies every longing of the glorified souls, in the light of the beatific vision, is giving himself to us in faith and mystery. It is the same thing. It seems to me that I have found my heaven on earth, since heaven is God and God is in my soul. The day I understood that, everything became clear to me and I wish I could whisper this secret to those I love in order that they also might cling closely to God through everything, and that Christ's prayer might be fulfilled: 'Father. . . . that they may be made perfect in one.' "[8] (Jn 17:21–23)

She knew, in the solitude of her soul, intimacy with God, which compelled her to speak: "I feel so much love upon my soul; it is like an ocean into which I plunge and lose myself. It is my vision on earth, while I await the vision face to face in Light. He is in me and I am in him. I have only to love him, to let myself be loved, at all times, in all circumstances. To awake in love, to move in love, to sleep in love, my soul in his soul, my heart in his Heart, that I may be purified and delivered from my miseries by contact with him."[9]

Fruitfulness in the Spirit

This matured intimacy with God, as a seedbed for endless progeny, is to the believing person the most generative of all activities. One act of pure love is of more value than all works put together, as John of the Cross teaches. Born from the person whom God has claimed in solitude is a heritage greater than the sands on a seashore. The waves of transformative union with God have washed to the shore of God countless souls, the fruit of divine/human intimacy in solitude. The person, now steeped in contemplative love, flowing from union with God, becomes astonishingly fruitful for the church and the salvation of all people. Humbled, forgetful of self, and enthusiastic for God, the person runs the way of zealous evangelization in a relatively faithless world. God has a magnificent desire to make us fruitful sharers in the mystery of salvation and in the holiness of God's people!

The desire that all people come to know, love, and serve God flares repeatedly within the person transformed by love, reaching to whomever will welcome the good news of Jesus. The person of faith is by nature an apostle, one sent to proclaim, if only by one's life, the gospel of peace, love, and forgiveness. As in all growth in life, branches and leaves spring from little seeds and gradually unfold to blossom. Eventually, they produce the fruits of a good harvest. "The kingdom of heaven is like a mustard seed that someone took and sowed in his field; it is the smallest of all seeds, but when it has grown it is the greatest of shrubs and becomes a tree, so that the birds of the air come and make nests in its branches" (Mt 13:31–32). In the end, God's work will not be hindered; life will triumph; love will reign; glory will come forever, to those who believe, who hope, and who love.

Elizabeth of the Trinity would daringly pray: "Consuming Fire, Spirit of Love, come down upon me and make me as it were an incarnation of the Word; may I be another humanity in which he lives out once more his mystery. And you, Father, bend down to your poor little creature, cover her with your shadow and see in her only the Well-Beloved in whom you were well pleased."[10]

Such is the intimacy flowing from the solitude of God.

Chapter 5

Prayer in Solitude

Much has been said of prayer in the context of the previous chapters. Now I will center on more passive prayer and the meaning of incessant prayer, since these are prevailing in a life in solitude. "Pray in the Spirit at all times in every prayer and supplication." (Eph 6:18)

By passive prayer, I mean that inflow of God's light, life, and love that is purely God's gift of himself to us. We are seekers who cannot procure the gift save by humble reception. The initiative is God's. I also refer, in a lesser way, to passive prayer as those forms of prayer that have reduced activity on our part: prayer of quiet or recollection, prayer of simple regard, prayer of abandonment, prayer of suffering or endurance. These often precede our preparation for God's gift of contemplative prayer.

In solitude, one moves freely in and out of these many dwellings of prayer without identifying or analyzing the changes. I may know I am praying by my efforts to be attentive to God's presence, but then what I know is that I am striving to pray. I am waiting on God. The actual prayer begins when the thoughts become a loving forgetfulness of self and what is going on, and a surrender to the God in whom I am a prayer. Later, after the experience, the person knows it was not he or she who was praying. God's wind in the person's sails carried the person away. These moments may not be frequent and really cannot be constant due to our human condition; however, this does not mean prayer ends.

Prayer takes another form, a new shape, as the rhythm of the waves makes new peaks when the wind and the tide press upon them. Prayer effuses out of life from the normal sway of thought, mood, feeling, impact—the impression of what happens to us from moment to moment. Nothing can prevent the person who prays from meeting God. Hers is a receptivity to God's prime desire: to give God's self to us through excessive goodness and love. The human spirit thrives on God's life within. This prayer integrates the whole person.

So my laughing, dying, sighing, and singing are my prayer when God is my love. My whistling, dancing, gazing, and gasping are my prayer when God is my love. My agonizing, enduring, struggling, and suffering are my prayer when God is my love. Nothing is excluded as a prayer to the God in whom I live and move and have my being.

John of the Cross writes beautifully of this as a prerequisite for inner solitude: "whether you eat or drink, or speak or converse with lay people, or do anything else, you should always do so with the *desire for God and with your heart fixed on Him*." [1] (italics mine)

Incessant prayer is about desire. Incessant prayer speaks of love that never ends. In the inner solitude of our own felt poverty, our own sinfulness, our own incessant helplessness, unceasing prayer perdures, quietly, gently as the still depths of an ocean. "The Spirit helps us in our weakness; for we do not know how to pray as we ought, but that very Spirit intercedes with sighs too deep for words." (Rom 8:26)

Desire, longing, yearning fill the heart fixed on God. God has implanted this desire in our heart. God knows we desire to respond to his love. Aware of the frailty of our human nature,

God enables us, through grace, to participate in divine life, to live as Jesus has shown, to love in self-giving. We are assured by St. John of the Cross: "If anything pleases Him [God], it is the exaltation of the soul. Since there is no way by which He can exalt her more than by making her equal to Himself, He is pleased only with her love."[2]

A person's prayer is the desert solitude in which God communicates to her or him. When our prayer feels like a desert wasteland or wilderness, Christ reveals to us our complete dependence upon God. When, in solitude, Christ becomes our prayer and our revelation, we are carried by the divine Spirit deeper into the mystery of love giving itself. When charity burns in the *desert heart* of a person, solitude is a trysting place for lovers, the milieu of consummate union. A hidden, secret union; nonetheless, very real.

We were fashioned with a transcendent capacity for union with God, no matter how often we tend to flaw this gift by sin and lack of response. At the core of our being, a cry emerges day and night, moment by moment, now and forever, "You are my God; it is you whom I seek." God incessantly responds, "You shall have your desire, according to your faith."

There is a story told about a woman who prayed each day, "God enable me to do great works for you. Help me to serve you with ardent generosity. This love I desire to give to you." She heard God say to her, "Strive each day to fulfill your desire; serve with love." So this she did, day after day, caring for others, working diligently, giving herself in deeds of love. She would pray each day, "this love I desire to give to You." Then one day she became very ill and could not move from her bed, although she continued her prayer, "this love I desire to give to you." After many days and weeks of illness and weakness, she pleaded to God, "I can no longer serve; I have no strength; how can I give you my love?" The Lord assured her, "it is enough to desire it."

Prayer and Diminishment

All that happens in prayer includes a dying process. Death is no foreigner to the person who prays; death is, by virtue of prayer, a necessity inherent to the process of transformation by love in Christ. Both the martyr and the mystic face death and accept it. As a Zen master would say, one should sit in meditation as though someone were standing in front of you with a sword ready to kill at one stroke. So the mystic looks at death with eyes open, knowing the passageway to life is no other than through death. The mystic seeks the grace to repress or deny nothing. The inner demons need to surface and to be looked at, that they may be released. Then God must be faced—a more devastating experience of death, the void of total death, even the void of God in one's life, or so it seems. "O death, where is your victory? O death, where is your sting?" (I Cor 15:55)

John of the Cross affirms the necessity of this passage through death in these words: "It is fitting that the soul be in this sepulcher of dark death in order that it attain the spiritual resurrection for which it hopes."[3] St. Paul presents it this way: "He will transform the body of our humiliation that it may be conformed to the body of his glory." (Phil 3:21)

Jesus, in Gethsemane, knew this mystic death before he went to Calvary. His humanity bore the horrendous weight of sin and its consequences, the cost of redemption that seeped from the body of Jesus in drops of blood. This blood of life-giving sacrifice would splash upon the whole world as death took its complete toll and was conquered by an undying love that turned death into life. "Jesus emptied himself taking the form of a slave. . . . And being found in human form, he humbled himself and became obedient to the point of death—even to death on a Cross." (Phil 2:7–8)

Prayer When God Seems Gone

Having spoken of the Presence/Absence of God in prayer in Chapter Two, I need mention now only the experience of estrangement when solitude seems to veil God in a prayer that seems foreign and nonexistent. I cannot connect with God in the times we are alone. Even the thought of a "dark night" erases any feeling of contact or presence. It seems that God is a stranger, or I am a stranger to him. My faith is alive but any sense or thought of nearness has vanished, and I am crying, "Are you there?" "Do you recognize me?"

I am reminded of a beautiful story of an elderly man who went for an early doctor's appointment and remarked to the nurse, when his wait grew lengthy, "I have a meeting in another place at 9:00 a.m. I may have to leave in order to be there." The nurse, seeing his concern, asked him, "It must be a very important appointment you will be having?" The man replied, "Yes, very important. I am meeting my wife, as I do every day, for breakfast. She is in an Alzheimer's unit in the nursing home. She does not know who I am." The nurse responded, "You have breakfast with your wife each day, and she does not know who you are?" "Yes," said the gentlemen, "but I know who she is."

When at prayer, I wait, like the wife, for my "unknown visitor," God is there. When I feel that I do not know God and he is a "stranger" to me, it can be consoling to recall that God, like the faithful husband in the story, knows who I am: his beloved. When we keep our morning rendezvous of prayer each day, God is faithful to visit us. He knows who we are. We move from the devastating solitude of "unknowing" to the creative solitude of being known and loved.

Being-In-Love

William Johnston, in his book *Letters To Contemplatives* tells in exquisitely simply terms of another form of passive prayer, that of just being:

> "There is a Christian contemplative prayer of just being. One simply sits in the Presence of God, aware that one is enveloped in this immense love which fills the universe. No words are necessary. No thinking is necessary. In this contemplative prayer my being becomes being-in-love."[4]

Johnston relates this prayer to the unrest of the world in its quest for peace by saying:

> "Now we will establish peace, not only by doing but also, and more importantly, by being. If more and more people can BE in the Presence of God, if more and more people can allow their being to become being-in-love, if more and more people can let their consciousness expand lovingly to all men and women, to the whole environment and to the limitless universe—if we can experience the enormous power of being-in-love, then we will be on the royal road to peace."[5]

It can be prayed, "My God, you are always with me. When I am with you, I am a *being in Love.*" Yes, prayer is a being-in-Love, remaining in the Love who is God. God gives me being, and I am most myself when I abide in God as a being-in-Love. God reveals me to myself. God reveals himself to me. God instructs me to know that God is God, and there is no other. The human heart wants to lift its praise to God for this wondrous truth!

The most consoling revelation about love is that God is love *poured out to us* and, when welcomed, *poured into us* by God's indwelling Holy Spirit (Rom 5:5). We become love by participation. Being-in-Love becomes being a lover whose love is "sourced" by and shared with God. I love with the very love of God, all a total gift! Here prayer is a way of life; it is true life itself; it has become incessant prayer. One lives as a drop of water in a fountain flowing from the side of Christ, bathed always in this living water so as to become more like him, every day, poured out in love.

In pondering the indwelling presence of God in our graced existence, we come to see a truth that both baffles and delights us. God lives in us; we live in God. God gives divine life to us as to those who do not have it; we receive life from God as a gift and then have a life to give back to God. God loves us and gives us love as to those who do not have love; we receive love and then have love to give back to God in return. Tremendous mystery of divine munificence! All is from God, even our gift to God. Wonderful exchange.

Without our knowledge, prayer continues and rests like a sleeping baby even when we are convinced that prayer has ceased. It can be stirred to awakening whenever we turn to

God and surrender to the Holy Spirit. Then new cries of need for nurturing and comfort call to God, and resumed is the tender flow of love between a child and Mother, lover with Beloved. The divine friendship ignites at each new encounter. Little by little, I am becoming a prayer, unceasing.

The mystic St. Catherine of Siena prayed from her heart: "Eternal God, eternal Trinity. . . . You are a mystery as deep as the sea; the more I search, the more I find, and the more I find the more I search for you. But I can never be satisfied; what I receive will ever leave me desiring more."[6]

Chapter 6

Solitude's Savorings

Ideally, one does not enter solitude for self gain, although the benefits are myriad and consequential. One does not enter solitude, realistically, without awareness that the experience may hold no visible fruits, although these will undoubtedly be present. One enters solitude to have a deepened love relationship, a union with God. Whenever that happens, ripples of concentric circles of personal and apostolic value flow out naturally, as when a pebble is tossed into the river. Solitude has its "savorings."

Can one seek the living God without savoring his goodness? Does the touch of divine love leave unchanged the recipient of that arrow? Has fire no mark to leave? Solitude's savorings are transformative, like the sun's rays that change whatever they rest upon. Some effects burn profoundly deep with lasting gifts of true joy, genuine humility, quiet peace, and gentle love. The human heart expands in inclusive compassion for others, nonintrusive understanding, and holy wisdom, as is manifest in the gift of poverty of spirit. Traces of hypocrisy, pretense, masking, and falsehood melt before the burning presence of divine love. The person in solitude sees, hears, tastes, and touches the One to whom he or she is to return, and with whom he or she will share eternal life, which has already begun here on earth.

Joy

Joy, a fruit of solitude, has a unique flavor of having been planted so deeply in the person's spirit that it permeates one's entire being with a sense of wonder and delight, a sense of well-being and rightness even amidst suffering. This joy exists, unperturbed, even when one is in deepest sorrow. It can be described as that true gladness in the depth of one's spirit; the experience of sheer goodness, God touch as the soul and the person delights in the gift.

Humility

Humility, another fruit of solitude, runs restfully over rocks of resistance to trickle into lakes of truth, even amidst the sharp sight of one's weaknesses and sins. This gift of humility, to walk in the truth and to know one's place before God, shares the gift of joy in the munificence of God, the giver. We read in *The Spiritual Canticle* of St. John of the Cross of mutual surrender in mystical marriage and of God's amazing love: "In this interior union God communicates Himself to the soul with such genuine love that no mother's affection, in which she tenderly caresses her child, nor brother's love, nor friendship is comparable to it. The tenderness and truth of love by which the Father favors and exalts this humble and loving soul reaches such a degree—O wonderful thing, worthy of all our awe and admiration—that the Father Himself becomes subject to her for her exaltation as though He were her servant and she His lord. And He is as solicitous in favoring her as He would be if He were her slave and she His god. So profound is the humility and sweetness of God!"[1] This would seem unbelievable if we were we not to walk in the truth we share of the humility of God. The humble person knows this wonder and praises God unceasingly. The truth has set her free.

Peace

The precious gift of peace found in solitude is the overall well-being and harmony of order, which burrows painstakingly into the recesses of a person's spirit to penetrate and permeate the soil of one's substance with God's refreshing wholeness. This peace prevails, even in circumstances of suffering, darkness, and pain. It is the deep stillness at the ocean's bottom when waves hurl and toss above. Peace is a hallmark of solitude's gifts. It reveals the integration of the whole person, which is taking place in gradual increments toward ultimate completion. "Peace, I leave with you; my peace I give to you. Do not let your hearts be troubled, and do not let them be afraid." (Jn 14:27)

Of all fruits, charity is the queen. This gentle love, which floods the person and comprises the whole meaning of a life in solitude with God, has ripened in generous self-giving. It deserves a chapter in itself, which will follow in Chapter Eight.

A Full Heart

The person who savors solitude knows that solitude's way is one of enlargement. In it the heart can expand in freedom, thus characterizing solitude's purpose: to let the heart grow in receptivity to God's love. The full heart must, of basic necessity, include everyone in its compassion. The person is compelled to give acceptance—and "give" is the salient word—to every-one. The dweller in solitude, now overwhelmed by love, has no desire to exclude a single person from his love and prayer, because he has tasted the bittersweet reality of his own poverty and need for love. One knows why Jesus prayed, "Father, as you are in me and I am in you, may they also be in us, so that the world may believe that you have sent me. The glory that you have given me I have given them, so that they may be one, as we are one, I in them and you in me, that they may become completely one" (Jn 17:21–23). The "full heart" symbolizes the boundless openness of a person who, knowing she has received all from God, welcomes everyone into her heart full of love.

Pretense

What then of hypocrisy, pretence, masking, falsehood? How can they even be mentioned in solitude's environs? These are incompatible, simply because in solitude there is nothing to hide and nowhere to cover oneself. The desert is no place for masquerades. Even pain is turned into suffering love. Sincerity and genuineness prevail. One stands exposed in the faced reality of the truth of who one is. The door opens for liberating freedom. We are no longer held bound to slavish needs for esteem, adulation, admiration, or human respect. The self is occupied with God's praise, God's glory, God being loved. The heart has been filled to overflowing, as water bubbling up from one's innermost being. "The water I will give will become in them a spring of water gushing up to eternal life." (Jn 4:14)

Wilderness Therapy

It is pertinent and interesting to see, in our day, the healing effects of solitude and community in the lives of very seriously disturbed young adults who partake of what is known as "wilderness therapy." These young men and women—chemically addicted, suicidal, angry, and depressed—have passed through myriad testing programs, numerous counseling sessions, imprisonment, and hospitalization with little lasting help for their deeply painful, futile ways of coping with fear, self-hatred, sexual aberrations, and aggressive rebellion. They have tried every sort of survival mechanism they could create.

Gary Ferguson, in his book *Shouting At The Sky*, graphically tells the story of men and women who, in the wilderness and supervised with uncompromising discipline in a supportive community, are placed in an environment where survival depends upon their own resourcefulness, endurance, and persistent efforts to live in the mountains, forests, and canyons of Utah. Their required "solos" in the wilderness bring them face-to-face with the rugged and life-threatening wild, where they must rely upon their learned skills to make a fire, scramble for food, and dig for water to satisfy their basic needs. All this in the forest, where coyotes, bears, and other ferocious animals wander freely!

A greater challenge they must face honestly lies within: the inner demons, the repressed or expressed anger, the desperate fight for personal acceptance and worth, and the endless search for the healing of compulsions. They seek wholeness and meaning. As one participant described it, we "had to process stuff, how to approach problems, how to tell the truth. . . . There was no place to hide. Sooner or later you had to work on your stuff. That's one of the things that scares me about going home; back there it's so easy to disappear."[2]

The wilderness, the desert, or entry into any kind of solitude is a place of testing and transformation. To take responsibility for one's life, to endure persistently, to face reality is to find oneself emerging more humble, more grateful, and freer to live in the truth. One learns to accept one's place with God and others after first accepting oneself as one is, even, perhaps, without much significant change. Solitude enables the person to present himself before God, look into the mirror of his or her own truth, and begin to make the choices that will lead to healing. Christ's love does transform the person who bears Christ's image. The savorings of solitude run deep into transformative truth. From the wilderness, a chastened person has emerged.

Playfulness

Can we say that in solitude one may be released to the gift of playfulness? What place has playfulness in the quiet of solitude? Who is the new person transformed in solitude? Here the child of wonder, whose innocent joy and light-hearted freedom coalesce on the playground of God's manifold creation, emerges purified, to her delight. Playfulness is not a performance that begins and ends. It becomes a habitual attitude of life. Playfulness, in a Christian sense, is not a game to be won or a competition in which to be engaged; even less, is it "playing a make-believe part." Playfulness is entering into the Wisdom of God—enjoying the freedom of the children of God.

The revelation of beauty surrounds every person. We can enjoy our playmate, Wisdom, who delights in the children of human beings. Contrastingly, we also live in a world where poverty, inequality, injustice, and deprivation dispossess people of their basic human dignities. How does one play amidst these? I suggest playfulness is the ability to live in the real here-and-now with a heart that explores, a heart that trusts God's goodness—to admit what is and then strive to approach everything with childlike trust and mature faith in the loving designs of God, who is always working good. With God, all things are possible. With God, all things shall be well. With God, crooked lines are eventually straightened or reconfigured. Playfulness enables us to participate in God's mirth and to transform the ordinary into moments of grateful joy, because God has graced us with every blessing from above. God delights in human beings.

The mature wisdom of insight that has aged in solitude leaves the person as innocent as a child. God smiles and you smile. God laughs with you and you laugh back in delight. It is a laughter of complete acceptance of oneself and all that is, as it is. You are free to play as hard and as long as you want if your heart stays young in the presence of God. All action and labor, all struggle and effort, all weariness and fatigue are also part of the play, because it is all part of a life of love unfolding in God's presence and providence. We need only welcome what is and let it teach us.

Even suffering and pain, endured in love, have a place in playfulness. One endures these circumstances with glad acceptance, as a "wounded clown." April's Fool was Christ crucified, his death absurdity. The resurrection hailed Christ's triumph and we, who believe, sing the alleluia song of play-fulness and exalted joy. I believe in the resurrection. I believe God has power to raise the dead. God has done this and will continue to do this until the end of time. It is the child of God who lives this mystery with a playful heart.

Chapter 7

Solitude's Sufferings

Suffering is not a favorite conversational subject. Often we would rather be silent about it because we hear so many people complain of their sufferings, and we too feel guilty because we ourselves are among the chief complainers. Perhaps I am speaking more of myself, because there are others who bear their burdens generously and without murmuring. These are the saints of our day.

I believe anyone who attempts to write about suffering surely knows it is a volatile endeavor—prone to many interpretations and some misunderstandings. Who can know the mind of another? "I the Lord test the mind and search the heart, to give to all according to their ways, according to the fruit of their doings." (Jer 17:10)

One person's anxious and devastating suffering is another's daily diet, borne with patient acceptance. One person's intense pain is another's light burden of love. One person can endure physical suffering that another finds unbearable, while the former could not well endure the psychological pain of the latter. Nonetheless, everyone knows some form of discomfort, pain, anguish, loss, or deprivation, which each terms "suffering." Said another way, every person has something to undergo, to endure, to bear, to accept, or to tolerate. How we cope with whatever suffering is ours makes a difference in its effect upon us. There is a purpose to these experiences. Suffering is a veritable necessity for human growth.

Are these experiences aggravated in solitude? Sometimes. Is there a form of suffering particularly present when one spends time alone with God? Most probably, if one is faithful in seeking God in solitude. What is to be learned through humble acceptance of the suffering that is ours and its consequences? Precious much! One learns, primarily, the ways of God, the likeness to Jesus in his Paschal mystery, the part one is to fulfill in the "filling up of the sufferings of Christ" (Col 1:24), the ways of true love. One learns the depth of one's own poverty, weakness, and helplessness. One comes to understand that without God one cannot do anything! One cannot even be. One learns a multitude of little things, which serve to enlighten the staid and cemented ways that restrain us from loving as God loves.

God is no timid lover. God will not settle for anything less than our complete transformation in love, whatever it may entail. What it does entail depends upon three primary conditions: what needs to be purified; how generously we respond to our transformation process; and what mission God has given us to accomplish in the world.

God is infinitely patient. How long it takes is not as important as the process itself: intimate union with God all along the way. God will not coerce our will, but God waits upon our willingness to respond. God can wait, infinitely, for our readiness to listen and to consent. Whatever God does is loving. We need to discover this love in everything that happens. Always, God wants only our good, or as St. John of the Cross says to our astonishment, our exaltation. That can be a frightening truth for us. We need to approach it from the perspective of God's infinite benevolence. God wants our complete and eternal happiness. God wants to be that for us. What does this process of sanctification look like in the real of life?

Timing

Timing is an important necessity in the process of our sanctification: a time for pruning and a time for refraining from pruning—our own particularly; a time suited for sacrifice and a time when sacrifice must wait; a time for fathoming depths and a time to dig no deeper; a time for self-emptying and a time for compassionate mercy on ourselves; a time to use all one's strength and a time to let one's weaknesses call for help; a time to weep and repent and a time to give oneself humble respite; a time when God will move quickly because of our generosity and a time when a snail's pace is better and more merciful.

As timing varies, one goal is constant: to share Christ's life, means, eventually, sharing in the passion, death, and resurrection of Jesus Christ. To evade these may be temporarily possible, but sooner or later they must be approached. To choose to engage in these realities and to participate fully calls for prayer, trust in God, and loving union with God's will for each of us.

When God calls a person into solitude, however long or short a time, the courage is extended to meet this invitation. It is a kairos moment of grace. Somehow we know that the timing is right, and it is now. I have a friend who told me he knows every ten years something "big" is going to take place, and it usually involves extensive pain and eventual growth. He has seen a pattern in his life. God knows what he needs and when to ask more. "The more God wants to give, the more demanding he makes our desires" is St. John of the Cross's way of saying that if God gives you the desire to grow in union with him, the more graces you will be given to facilitate this growth.

A person shared with me what she recognized on her journey, "Oh, I knew it would cost; I prayed for grace and then plunged into the waters of dying and rebirth," an extension of the plunging, through baptism, into the death of Christ. Resurrection would come later. This person discovered her choice to flow with the grace was one of the most important decisions of her life. The consequent experiences of growth ensued beyond imagining. This transformation is radical and still growing in her life. There is a time when "plunging into the waters" is our decision toward conversion. It is the "time," the "hour" of our personal place in salvation history.

The Thicket

When one is willing to enter into solitude in a constant and faithful search for union with God enkindled by love for Jesus Christ, then the holy and life-giving Spirit of Abba and of Jesus will lead the pilgrim over trackless paths into the "thicket of God." St. John of the Cross calls this thicket "the delectable wisdom of God."[1]

"This thicket," John says, "into which the soul thus wants to enter also signifies very appropriately the thicket and multitude of trials and tribulations, for suffering is very delightful and beneficial to her. Suffering is the means of her penetrating further, deep into the thicket of the delectable wisdom of God. The purest suffering brings with it the purest and most intimate knowing, and consequently the purest and highest joy, because it is a knowing from further within."[2]

The deepest cellar of darkness and suffering, no matter how painfully we each experience it, breeds the seeds of new light and transforming grace when our faith begins to recognize the pattern of darkness to light, of pain to freedom, of the cross to the resurrection. Both must be present and endured: one follows another, as birth follows conception, after a long preparation of gestation and development.

The thicket holds a multitude of God's splendid works and profound judgments "that no matter how much the soul knows, she can always enter it further; it is vast and its riches incomprehensible."[3] Consequently, the gate into the thicket of these "riches of God's wisdom is the cross which is narrow, and few desire to enter by it, but many desire the delights obtained from entering these."[4]

This desire for God will bring both the joy and the pain of letting God have his way in our lives. From the beginning, the human person, created in God's image and likeness, was magnificently graced with a capacity for God. Something was given to human beings, as to no other work of creation, which innately and necessarily consumes a person with longing for God. There is no true fulfillment until that person is brought into consummate union with the blessed Trinity, a life she has begun to share here on earth. Simply said, we are made for God and to enjoy God. This precious desire will not rest, nor will it be annihilated even if we want to smother it for a long time. "Why are you cast down, O my soul, and why are you disquieted within me? Hope in God; for I shall again praise him, my help and my God" (Ps 43:5). "My whole being cries out for the living God."

When we, drawn by God, venture into the thicket, we will move from God to God to more of God—endlessly. Even in eternal life, we will discover God endlessly. How else could we explain the inexhaustibility of God, the eternal infinitude?

What delays this union that the Infinite God desires with us and we, as finite beings, desire? Precisely this: the disproportion of the two, the total contrast between God's loving and ours, the unlikeness of the two manners of loving. "Two contraries cannot coexist in the same subject. Darkness, an attachment to creatures, and light, which is God, are contraries and bear no likeness toward each other. . . . Consequently, the light of divine union cannot be established in the soul until these affections are eradicated." John of the Cross continues: "an attachment to a creature makes a person equal to that creature; the firmer the attachment, the closer is the likeness to the creature and the greater the equality. For love effects a likeness between the lover and the object loved."[5]

This is why a transformation must take place. Our unlikeness to God is changed more and more until God shines forth in all our ways. We are in desperate need of liberation, because our selfishness, our pleasure-seeking, our sinfulness has estranged us from God in a bondage that must be broken. Otherwise, there cannot be the freedom to love as God loves. The innate longing we have is insatiable, except by God. We are destined to love in and with and through God.

St. Teresa of Jesus laments, "I cannot help but feel very sorry to see what we lose through our own fault. Even though it is true that these are blessings the Lord gives to whomever He wills, His Majesty would give them all to us if we loved Him as He loves us. He doesn't desire anything else than to have those to whom to give. His riches do not lessen when He gives them away."[6]

Liberation

What if we were to believe that God's will is our liberation to love, that God wants, passionately, to free us from all obstacles for this experience of union with him? What then would become of our godly plans to serve God, which really serve ourselves? What would become of our carefully discerned and cautiously decided works of service to others that do not respect them, nor are God's ways for them? What would happen to our complacency in prayer, our rightly respected acts of devotion often recited to self-gratify our so-called fidelity to obligations, while avoiding the true worship of God in spirit and truth and love for others? "Woe to you, scribes and Pharisees, hypocrites! For you tithe mint, dill and cummin and have neglected the weightier matters of the law: justice and mercy and faith." (Mt 23:23)

Oh, happy night that presages the dawn! If we were to trust God and entrust ourselves to God completely, the result would be greater openness to God revealing himself more truly, unencumbered by our biases and prejudices. We would see new things, in new ways, with a responsiveness freeing us for new possibilities. Blessed are your eyes that now see what others long to see and which God reveals to the simple-hearted.

Like children, we pile block upon block of self-imposed burdens, which topple before one light touch of God's will for us and leave us either saddened by the demise of our works or gladdened by the new creation that is soon to come by God's hand, in another way. Oh, happy day when God's liberation brings us into a mature, living faith.

The Sentence of Death

One day, the transformative process will give entry into another kind of suffering. I tremble to approach it, precisely because it is entirely God's handiwork and beyond human efforts. It is what Teresa of Jesus speaks of in the sixth dwelling place of *The Interior Castle* and John of the Cross explains in the fourth stanza of *The Living Flame of Love* and the second book of *The Dark Night*. It is similar to what St. Paul describes in his Second Letter to the Corinthians 1:8–9: "For we were so utterly, unbearably crushed that we despaired of life itself. Indeed, we felt we had received the sentence of death so that we would rely not on ourselves but on God who raises the dead."

In terms John of the Cross would use for this inner torment, there takes place "an oppressive undoing"[7] of the person whom God takes through the dark night of spirit. It is necessary for this transformation in love to transpire, because "Suffering produces endurance, and endurance produces character and character produces hope, and hope does not disappoint us." (Rom 5:3–5)

This "undoing" needs to be addressed, because of its essential resemblance to the dying and rising of Christ that is the model for our lives. It is a passage many are called to traverse in this earthly life. We know of it in the lives of the saints.

St. John of the Cross explains: "When this purgative contemplation oppresses a man, he feels very vividly indeed the shadow of death, the sighs of death and the sorrows of hell, all of which reflect the feeling of God's absence, of being chastised and rejected by Him, and of being unworthy of Him, as well as the object of His anger. The soul experiences all this and even more, for now it seems that this affliction will last forever."[8] John of the Cross speaks of the experience in its extreme: "These are the ones who go down into hell alive since their purgation on earth is similar to that of purgatory."[9]

The ultimate liberation taking place is from the deep-rooted attachment and tenacity we have to our own will and identity, *as our own*. It is the antithesis of God's words through St. Paul, "You are not your own. . . . For you were bought with a price; therefore glorify God in your body." (I Cor 6:19–20)

This is a liberation also from the supreme sin of pride and possessiveness, in our hidden depths, our wanting to be chief directors of our own lives. Assenting to this fallacy of pride is a misuse of the precious gift of our free wills, which are ordained to be surrendered to God as our sole master, savior, and beloved. "When you were younger, you used to fasten your own belt and to go wherever you wished. But when you grow old, you will stretch out your hands and someone else will fasten a belt around you and take you where you do not wish to go." (Jn 21:18)

The extent of our possessiveness as arbiters of our destiny is insidious and deceptive. Indeed, it is impossible to prevent its pervasive influence upon our lives, except by the grace of God in the dark night of the purification of the spirit, initiated and completed by God alone. This dispossession or detachment is a radical replacement of one's own operations by the Holy Spirit of God, who becomes supreme mover and inspirer in the fulfillment of God's will in the person so transformed. The person is living in habitual surrender to the divine good pleasure, as that which is her sole desire. This desire, being from God and stirred within the person, is being fulfilled in the *transformation* of the person, a veritable death and rebirth.

The person loses all that she sought to be. The experience is a grieving as in death, as in the seeming annihilation of self. In reality, what is transpiring in this experience of supposed annihilation is a *radical transfiguration*, so that she no longer lives, but Christ lives in her (Gal 2:20). She has passed beyond knowing herself as she was. God breathes, moves, directs, and inspires all she does. The life of God is her life.

In the commentary on *The Spiritual Canticle*, John of the Cross, describes the verse "I lost myself, and was found" in this way: "He who truly walks in love lets himself lose all things immediately in order to be found more attached to what he loves. On this account the soul affirms here that she lost herself. She achieved this in two ways: she became lost to herself by paying no attention to herself in anything, by concentrating on her Beloved and surrendering herself to Him freely and disinterestedly, with no desire to gain anything for herself; secondly, she became lost to all creatures, paying no heed to all her own affairs, but only to those of her Beloved. And this is to lose herself purposely, which is to desire to be found."[10]

What of God's part in this process? In *The Footprints of Love*, the authors explain an awesome reality, that "God loses himself in our loss of selfhood when our love loses the duplication of our self-awareness, our *making God an extension of ourselves* [italics mine]. Then, too, we discover our truest value, for it is reflected in God's eyes. In this way we actually become what God sees in us!"[11] This astounding truth reveals how completely God wants a union with us in the fullest participation a human being can have by sharing God's life on earth.

To become what God sees in us is to be the image of God's Son, Jesus Christ, made manifest. If the center of our soul

is God, as John of the Cross teaches, then this transformation is the splendor of baptism burgeoning like new growth
until its harvest is the splendid fulfillment of life in glory. Who
could believe in such love except that God has made it known
in Jesus Christ! What is asked of us in the process—and this is
a grace God alone can give—is that total abandonment of ourselves in cooperation with and surrender to the transforming
love of God.

> "I have abandoned and forgot myself
> Laying my face on my Beloved,
> All things ceased. I went out of myself,
> Leaving my cares
> Forgotten among the lilies."
>
> —DN, St. 8

Ecstasy—Out of Oneself

The person so surrendered to God feels as though the self has
passed over into God, and indeed it has. It is the intimacy of
nuptial union between spirit and Spirit. God, through the agonizing pain of the process of transformation—pain caused by
our sins and attachments, not God's intent—has released the
person from her own restrictions. What she could not do, God
has done and will continue to do in anyone willing to live by
faith in the mystery of the cross. As a priest and friend of mine
once remarked, "Our 'all too little' has been overwhelmed by
God's 'all too much.'" The desire for God has been subsumed
in God's desire for each person to be one in love with the Father,
Son, and Holy Spirit. The ecstasy of passing out of ourselves
into God implies a parting from self-preoccupation, so as to
pursue the good pleasure of the beloved. This is a form of true

ec-stasy, when one is taken out of oneself, as center stage, to a flight to God as true center of all one's being and activities.

"O souls who in spiritual matters desire to walk in security and consolation! If you but knew how much it behooves you to suffer in order to reach this security and consolation, and how, without suffering, you cannot attain to your desire, but rather turn back, in no way would you look for comfort either from God or from creatures. You would instead carry the cross. . . . You would consider it good fortune that, upon dying to this world and to yourselves, you would live to God in the delights of the spirit...you would merit that God fix His eyes on you and purge you more profoundly . . . in order to give you more interior blessings."[12]

"Lord, I know that your desires are right, that you afflicted me justly. Let your love be ready to console me by your promise to your servant" (Ps 119:75–76). Surprisingly, the person afflicted is not the only one "wounded." God also is wounded with love for the soul who loves God. How can this be? We turn to John of the Cross again for insight into this mystery.

The Wounded God

Living in the peace of God's magnificent work, the person knows:

> "in solitude He guides her,
> He alone, who also bears
> In solitude the wound of love."
>
> —SC, St. 35

The mystical doctor comments on this stanza: "That is, He [God] is wounded with love for the bride. The Bridegroom bears a great love for the solitude of the soul; but He is wounded much more by her love, since being wounded with love for Him, she desired to live alone in respect to all things. And He does not wish to leave her alone, but wounded by the solitude she embraces for His sake, and observing that she is dissatisfied with any other thing, He alone guides her, drawing her to and absorbing her in Himself. Had He not found her in spiritual solitude, He would not have wrought this in her.[13]

In loving us first, God chose to become vulnerable, to be wounded. Having given us unconditional, steadfast love, God accepts even our refusal to return this love. God will wait for us. Our desire for God, etched in the center of our being, needs to be nurtured, enlarged and receptive to the awesome reality that we are made for God and cannot rest until we rest in God, as St. Augustine made known.

This wound God experiences is not one of hurt, offense, or self-pity, as are many of our wounds, but a wound of love and by love. When we draw near to learn God's love and are moved by the Spirit of God to love in return, we so touch the heart of God as to wound it, so intensely does God desire our love. An astounding reality!

The solitude that no one can take away from a person is the "quietude of solitary love of her Spouse," as John of the Cross calls it. He continues, "there is no companionship which affords comfort to the soul that longs for God; indeed, until she finds Him, everything causes greater solitude."[14] Where formerly the person practiced the solitude of self-denial for her beloved in which she anguished because she was imperfect, "now she has built her nest in it [solitude] and has found refreshment and repose in having acquired it perfectly in

God."[15] God has become her dwelling place. The person has found a place in God where she can be satisfied; she has received the gift of solitude.

The Solitude of God

As was mentioned earlier, Saturday in Holy Week of the liturgical season can be described as the solitude of God, as lived and experienced in Jesus Christ.

The disciples were with him in Gethsemane when Jesus, troubled, voiced to Peter, James, and John, "I am deeply grieved, even to death; remain here and stay awake with me" (Mt 26:38). This prayer rang from his distressed and anguished heart, "my Father, if it is possible, let this cup pass from me; yet, not what I want but what you want." (Mt 26:39)

What immense solitude wrenched the being of Jesus when he asked Peter, "could you not stay awake with me one hour?" (Mt 26:40). Jesus longed for human companionship. Even Job's three friends, when they witnessed his intense suffering and diminishment, sat with him on the ground in silence "for seven days and seven nights. No one spoke a word to him, for they saw that his suffering was very great." (Job 2:13)

Silent presence between beloved friends rings quiet tones of solidarity and union of love as suffering is shared. Sometimes, no words are needed; they would tarnish the gold of silence. But Jesus was deprived of this comforting presence of friends, awake to his needs. The Son of Man, who was also Son of God, felt so abandoned that he cried out from the cross, "Father, why have you forsaken me?" (Mt 27:46). The solitude of Jesus is an abundant abyss of loving self-gift to the Father and to us. Jesus on the cross, abandoned, is the most intense "sounding solitude" ever to yield the fruit of salvation and resurrection for all people. This solitude sounds from east to west, from north to south and throughout the whole of creation, the fulfillment of the promise to us: "you shall never die." But die Jesus did—in solitude.

On Good Friday, after loving us to the end, Jesus commended his spirit to the Father, and gave up his spirit. The death of God! How can it be? Before this horrendous solitude of a mystery beyond human comprehension, a person, believing, prays "help my unbelief." Jesus was raised only after having truly died a human death, which brought to end his normal human bodily existence on this earth. He was then exalted above every other name, as the Risen Lord, whose body was now glorified.

On Holy Saturday, the church, in its liturgy, awaits that resurrection. Jesus was in the tomb, a hollowed rock of solitude where he had been laid, wrapped in a shroud with burial spices and herbs. A life apparently ended. The solitude of God! Is this what the saints experience who have traversed the road to Calvary in their own lives to enter the solitude of God? From death to *life*.

Beyond Suffering

From another perspective, Holy Saturday is also the most intense and imperative solitude of the human race. For the Christian believer, Jesus Christ is our only hope. The travelers to Emmaus voiced this when they said, "But we had hoped that he was the one to redeem Israel." (Lk 24:21)

Jesus lay in the tomb, the solitude of death, from which he would rise. Every tomb in which we feel dead is also a haven for resurrection. The tombs of the dead had already burst when Jesus died, as the scriptures tell us: "The earth shook, and the rocks were split. The tombs were opened and many bodies of the saints who had fallen asleep were raised." (Mt 27:51–52)

In the early hours of Holy Saturday morning, unseen, unheard, unknown to us, *Jesus Christ was raised from the dead*. Although there is no way to verify it, it is my belief that he went first to Mary, his mother—Mary, whose solitude was deepest next to that of Jesus. She held the greatest hope, and it would not be disappointed. Coming from the greatest solitude, like new growth in spring, Jesus was alive and glorified. Mary now knew what had been said: "and on the third day He will be raised from the dead" (Mt 16:21). What love and joy passed between Jesus and Mary when she beheld her risen Son! Here is the culmination of solitude. Here its sublime fruit: that perfect bliss with God through union with Christ Jesus in self-giving love.

Mary experienced what St. John of the Cross described of the person transformed in Christ, who, in the climax of a life of seeking God in solitude, has become that faithful spouse whose only activity is loving. "Having been made one with God, the soul is somehow God through participation. Although it is not God as perfectly as it will be in the next life, it is like the *shadow of God*. . . . the will of the two is one will, and thus God's operation and the soul's is one. Since God gives Himself with a free and gracious will, so too the soul, (possessing a will more generous and free the more it is united with God), gives to God, *God Himself in God*; and this a true and complete gift of the soul to God. . . . Because the soul in this gift to God offers Him the Holy Spirit with voluntary surrender, as something of its own (so that God loves Himself in the Holy Spirit as He deserves), it enjoys inestimable delight and fruition, seeing that it gives God something of its own, which is suited to Him according to His infinite being"[16] (italics mine). What a marvelous wonder: God so exalting the human person!

Mary, Jesus' mother, had given herself totally to the Holy Spirit at the Annunciation. She was the temple of the Holy Spirit within which God conceived the Word-made-flesh. The Blessed Virgin returned to God that very Spirit of love in every moment of her self-giving. Hers was the most intimate, complete, and acceptable offering of a human person, next to Jesus, her Son. Now she, as Jesus also, was beyond suffering. Darkness had passed and a new morn was here. The victory was won; the price of pardon paid; a new creation emerged. The Lord is truly risen, Alleluia! Mary now sings with the angels: Glory to God in the highest!

Chapter 8

Love Is All the Meaning

"For this is the message you have heard from the beginning, that we should love one another."

—I Jn 3:11

Were I to presume to speak, comprehensively, of love's meaning, I would be a fool who sought to capture the sky in a plastic bag. Love's story is as vast and limitless as there are people who fall in love and stay in love. The mystery is as magnificently beautiful and precious as God sending his Son to become a man, to die for us and to be raised from the dead to give us eternal life. The Jewish convert to Catholicism and Carmelite Nun, St. Teresa Benedicta of the Cross (Edith Stein), described love as "goodness giving itself away"[1]—she who herself gave her life for her people in the gas chambers of Auschwitz, in imitation of Jesus.

"He alone Who also bears
In solitude the wound of love."

—SC, St. 35

The mystical doctor, St. John of the Cross, says, "Love alone, which burns by soliciting the heart of the Beloved, is what guides and moves it (the soul) and makes it soar to God in an unknown way along the road of solitude."[2]

How do I love you, my God, in these multitudes of vary-
ing solitudes? How do I, without refusing grace, let you love
me? When will love permeate my mind, heart, body, and soul,
so that Christ lives fully in me and, therefore, I am given to
others? Will you take, O merciful beloved, the empty solitude
of my heart and bring to it the fullness of your divine solitude,
so that love may reign? Here am I, Lord. I come to do your
will. These words, I suggest, could be love's prayer in solitude.
Immersed in trinitarian love, I learn the meaning of self-giving
love, God's love in me. One with Christ in doing whatever
God asks of me, I can live in any solitude, embraced by love.
Love is the meaning: God's love is present, filling every solitude. Ours is to recognize it and warmly welcome it.

Stories, of which the scriptures are full, are one way
to uncover, in life's simple beauties, the blinding rays of
God's unconditional, excessive love for human beings. Perhaps because God's love is so incomprehensible to us we
need to lighten the context in order to bear its burden of
godliness. Here is one story reflecting what was referred to in
a previous chapter.

A disciple once asked a wise monk who was praying
silently, "What are you doing?" The old monk, gently turning toward the disciple, answered, "I am being-in-love." "But
you are alone," said the disciple. "I am never alone," replied
the old monk. "Do you ever feel alone?" asked the disciple.
"Formerly, I did feel alone, frequently; but Jesus said, "I am
with you to the end of time." Since my being comes from God
and God is love, then whenever I turn to God, I am a being-in-
love. Also, when I choose to pray and remain in God's love, I
am being in love, for Jesus also said, "abide in my love."

God's love is an endless flow, like running waters, to every person and all that lives, because it is God's love that sustains all life. God's love moves within us and around us, as the Holy Spirit permeates the whole of creation and each one therein. Do we enter that flow or avoid it? Do we drink of that flow or refuse it? Do we submerge ourselves in that flow or flee in fear from the necessary suffering? How does solitude open to me this meaning of love?

Desire

The solitude that we are as human persons leaves us as vessels of receptivity, hungering for the love of God to fill us. God's love is his response to that desire planted in our hearts from eternity and from our conception and birth as children of God. The solitude that we are, our otherness, was given as a gift from God that God may lavish his profuse love on his creatures, as unique as they are. Our finiteness was meant to become, not a barrier, but a likeness and a union in that same God-love, the Holy Spirit, who is the bond between the Father and Son, yet equal to them. The Three in One, God's solitude-in-communion, have chosen to create and share their life. That life is a veritable avalanche of excessive love, a dispensing of God's life to all of us. Enough love to sustain each and every one of us in being from moment to moment. Increased love, when we welcome it, enables God to expand our intake. Transforming love, when the mystic becomes surrendered to the Holy Spirit, brings the *desire* into consummation.

This love is as climactic as ecstasy, meaning "out of oneself," and as generative and fruitful as the continuous flow of love from each life to a new life to another new life. Love, when refined by fire, "produces such likeness in this transformation of lovers that one can say each is the other and both are one."[3]

Refinement

There once was a woman who intently watched a silversmith as he held a piece of silver over the fire to let it become hot and ignite. He explained that the silver had to be held in the middle of the fire, where the flames were the hottest, to burn away all the impurities. She asked if the silversmith had to sit in front of the fire the whole time the silver was being refined. The man answered, yes, he not only had to sit there holding the silver, but he had to keep his eyes on the silver the entire time it was in the fire. If the silver was left there a moment too long, it would be destroyed.

"How do you know when the silver is fully refined?" the woman asked. "Oh," he replied, "that's easy—when I see my image in it." So it is when we are purified. God, the divine silversmith, can see his image in us—and so can others.

God's love is an unbroken circle from divine love, to divine-human love in Jesus Christ, to divine love shared with us in the Holy Spirit, to divine love returned from us to God. Gift to gift to Gift: God giving the Gift, which enables the recipient to give the Gift in return. It's all about loving.

We can drink, at any moment, of this love of God. This is not a "feeling" but a filling. The scriptures tell us this in myriad ways, one of which is St. Paul's words, "the love of God is poured into our hearts through the Holy Spirit that has been given to us." (Rom 5:5)

John of the Cross reiterates the same: "The soul that has reached this state of spiritual espousal knows how to do nothing else than love and walk always with its Spouse in the delights of love. Since in this state she has reached perfection, the form and nature of which, as St. Paul says, is love (Col 3:14) and since the more a soul loves the more completely it loves, this soul that is now perfect is all love, if one may express it so, and all her actions are love; she employs all her faculties and possessions in loving, giving up everything, like the wise merchant (Mt 13:44) for this treasure of love she has found hidden in God. She is conscious that love is so valuable in her Beloved's sight that He neither esteems nor makes use of anything else but love, and so she employs all her strength in the pure love of God desiring to serve Him perfectly . . . the soul easily extracts the sweetness of love from all the things that happen to her, that is, she loves God in them. Thus everything leads her to love."[4]

Every saint has left the same message as fruit of his or her own prayer and union with God. Such excessive benevolence and lavish outpouring of God in love to his creatures leaves us utterly overwhelmed with the beauty and goodness of God.

Love is the meaning of a return to solitude, where the call to transforming union with God in Christ is heard in the hearts of all lovers of him who first loved us. "God, who could not be considered paid with anything less, is considered paid with the gift of the soul; and he accepts it gratefully as something it gives him of its own. . . . a reciprocal love is thus actually formed between God and the soul like the marriage union and surrender, in which the goods of both . . . are possessed by both together."[5]

All that human beings were made for is being accomplished in the most delicate intimacy of union with God in love. According to John of the Cross, when God has enraptured the person in this intimacy, "the soul becomes God from God through participation in Him and in His attributes, which it terms the 'lamps of fire' . . . like the illumination that is within the very flames . . . transformed in them. It is like the air within the flame, enkindled and transformed in the flame, for the flame is nothing but enkindled air. . . . And the fire causes the air, which it has enkindled, to produce these same movements and splendors. . . . The movement of these divine flames . . . are not alone produced by the soul that is transformed in the flames of the Holy Spirit, nor does the Holy Spirit produce them alone, but they are the work of both the soul and Him. . . . Thus these movements of both God and the soul are not only splendors, but also glorification of the soul."[6]

One acts like God from within God in oneself! Love is the meaning of it all. Can there be any greater solitude than to wonder, uncomprehendingly, at the gracious excessiveness of God's love for us, unconditionally? Wait long in silence and wonder. Abide in that love, which is always available to you for the receiving. Then, as befits a lover, one can only sing praise, unceasingly.

"For a little of this pure love is more precious to God and the soul and more beneficial to the Church, than all the other works put together."[7]

Chapter 9

The Spirituality of Communion

"There is one Body and one Spirit just as you were called
to the one hope of your calling, one Lord, one faith, one
baptism, one God and Father of all, who is above all and
through all and in all."

—Eph 4:4–6

No human being is left untouched by a solitude that embodies
the loneliness, suffering, anguish, and pain of each person's
struggle to become inwardly free, to cope with the ambigui-
ties, burdens, and responsibilities of living with limits, weaknesses, and sinfulness. No mere human being can reach the
hidden suffering of another to identify and dispel it. But
another human of compassion and self-acceptance can *stand
by with empathy* as long as that person does not yield to being
a problem solver, a savior of the other—but rather, a person,
as Henri Nouwen says, "who reverently bow[s] before that
sacred empty space where God chose to lay down his broken
wounded body and from where he was raised up."[1]

There, in each one's personal solitude, uniquely one's own,
there, in poverty, alone and insecure, a person waits in peace
on the magnificently faithful, saving grace of our Savior, Jesus
Christ. With a constant and abiding faith, one can be confident in the hope that God fulfills his promises and that God
ordains all. Nonetheless, within the original solitude of each
person—entry impossible for another—there is also a desire

113

for union, a union with the Only One, and a union with all who are in communion with the Only One. Ingrained within our being is the godly desire to be at one with God and with everyone and with all that is. Our own integrity requires it. To be in communion is to be fulfilled.

In the previous chapter, where we saw love to be the meaning, lies the hint of a *spirituality of communion*. I suggest we look at solitude and communion from a perspective of four common experiences marking every person's life at one time or another:

The solitude of loss.

The solitude of poverty of spirit.

The solitude of each person's transformation process.

The solitude of each person's sanctification.

From that perspective of solidarity, we can see the soul-mate of solitude to be communion with everyone. We learn, alone with God, how to live with others; we learn from others how to turn to God. From solitude to communion to deeper solitude and deeper communion; it is the cycle of God's transforming activity.

Solitude of Loss

Loss is a devastating reality, with no immunity afforded by age, status, gender, time, or place. Loss, of necessity, is part of human living. Yet for some reason, we can refuse to accept it as part of "my" life. The story of Job in the scriptures is a litany of consecutive losses of sons, daughters, house, land, livestock, and so on. These did not end until the very body and person of Job was touched. Chided by his wife for his continual praise of God who "gives and takes away," Job sat in his misery, unwavering in faith. He sought understanding and was given only the awareness of his inability to understand. He put his mouth to the dust!

Alone, misunderstood, dejected, Job confronted God. His search for understanding, laden with a need to be able to "make things right," came to a finale when God starkly presented Job with the truth of the human inability to understand divine ways. One does not contend with God's wisdom without daring pride. Job humbly surrendered to the divine prerogative and understood he could not understand. He no longer needed to retrieve a loss that was for God's purposes. In solitude, Job saw more deeply into the meaning of Queen Esther's prayer, "Lord . . . help me, who am alone and have no helper but you." (Esth 14:3)

Although I may know loss in some form, I cannot fully know your loss. Each of us stands alone with that mystery. However, all of us share in the experience of loss with its multitude of sufferings and pain. When fear discloses our expectation of loss or harm, prayer in solitude brings us once more into the presence of God who, has power to create good from whatever happens and whose desire is to bring us to closer union with himself. When I name the loss, look it in the face with acceptance, allow it to teach me the truth of myself that I did not know before the loss, then, out of the seed of that solitude, emerges a new freedom and also a new poverty to be enriched spiritually.

Solitude of Poverty of Spirit

Having known the solitude of loss and experienced it many times, the seeker of God has a glimpse into a solitude that plumbs profoundly into one's own spirit, a solitude manifest in one's innate poverty. How readily we would shun the truth of our personal poverty! But it will not go away. We are gifted persons, with so high a calling that the Psalmist could say, "Yet you have made them a little lower than God" (Ps 8:5). We are endowed with talents, intelligence, imagination, and initiative to build robots to investigate other planets, to clone animals, to send jets into the air, and perhaps even one day to discover the yet elusive blessing of world peace. Yet we are all poor before God, others, and ourselves; that is, we are lacking in something. We are incomplete and unable to do many things we desire, eventually limited by illness and the final foe, death. This need not be discouraging for a Christian or any believer in God.

Jesus in the beatitudes praised the "poor in spirit" as those who shall claim "the kingdom of God." These *anawim* of God are those who know their need for God. These are they who, through personal pain, deprivation, and suffering, have it seared into their bones: their utter dependence upon God's grace for all they are and all they do. They are the happy ones who see their poverty as a blessing, because this awareness of need gently returns them to the arms of a loving Father in heaven.

I think the core of understanding poverty of spirit rests in *gladness of spirit*, the free abandonment to God from a center of poverty that delights confidently in God's loving care, trusting in his goodness. Think of a paraplegic who trusts his caregiver to be there and to prevent him from harm. He relies upon a love that is trustworthy. So do the poor in spirit, who surrender into the hands of a loving Father, knowing that those who ask, receive; those who seek, find; and to those who knock, it shall be opened to them.

Only a cheerful giver has truly penetrated into the poorness that is not destitution but blessing. In one's inner solitude lies the opportunity to surrender to the truth of human nature. In solitude we learn to love our humanness as a created beauty that is endearing to God whose beloved we are. Surely this is cause for joy. It has been said we become what God sees in us. We are valued because God has loved us, making us lovable and able to love in return.

Solitude of the Transformation Process

Poor in spirit, the person in quest of God, recognizes a transformation process weaving its way, sometimes secretly, through the lives of people who acknowledge and accept their personal poverty, painful as it may be. For some people, the transformation process is tediously long from one's first admission of a need for purification; through years of self-denial, labored virtue, detachment, and gradual surrender to the Holy Spirit; to its final stage when God initiates and accomplishes what could not be done by us. The loneliness, self-emptying, and generous yielding to God all along the way are like vast deserts through which the traveler experiences the barrenness of solitude, as well as a sense of loss and stripping that appear to leave one naked before God and oneself. The ego is dethroned; the self-emptying, extensive; the liberation from selfishness and pride, continuous; and the sense of loss, utterly depleting.

For others, the transformation process is shorter, but more intense, a purification by fire that resembles the solitude of the "fiery dart" piercing the heart of St. Teresa of Jesus or the nine-month solitary experience in a narrow, stuffy cell, which imprisoned St. John of the Cross in the confines of dark solitude and stripped him of sufficient nourishment, companionship, the sacraments, and physical necessities.

The more one allows God to work unhindered, the sooner and more continuous will be the transformation. Of whatever suffering is part of our purification process, no matter how painful, John of the Cross says to us: "How amazing and pitiful it is that the soul be so utterly weak and impure that the hand of God, though light and gentle, should feel so heavy and contrary. For the hand of God does not press down or weigh upon the soul, but only touches it, and this mercifully, for God's aim is to grant favors and not chastise it."[2]

What emerges from these experiences of profound solitude is a phoenix-like transfiguration, expanding the receiver's capacity for tremendously fruitful service to the church and one's neighbor. St. Teresa of Jesus founded numerable new monasteries of women and men before she died and expounded the ways of prayer in her written legacy. St. John of the Cross, in his mere forty-nine years, left us the heritage of his classic writings, the wisdom of his spiritual direction, and the witness of a life given totally to God in pure love.

Your and my transformation process may not yield notable external accomplishments, but the same workings within our mind, heart, and spirit will effect "a new heart and a new spirit." Together we become the work of art of the Holy Spirit that transforms the world. Truly this is solitude's progeny. I speak of holiness of life, affecting the salvation of others.

Solitude of Each Person's Sanctification

One of the most lonely and often unrecognized experiences of solitude is the "burden of holiness." To be made holy by that transforming process of self-emptying love and God's sanctifying ways is to become an image of Christ in his mysteries—and often a "crucified" image. The person, so transformed, is most likely unaware of the witness he or she gives to others and to the world. What is known more clearly is that they are "not of this world," but living very nearly and truly within God at the heart of the world with concern for all people. These purified and transparent persons radiate goodness, compassion, charity, and peace, while often "bearing the marks of Christ" in their bodies and spirit from the sufferings they endure in solitude. They experience both a deep and tender union with others and a lonely exile in their union with God. Their hearts burn with true charity and compassion for those who suffer. They feel in their entire being the consequences of sin in their own lives and in those of others. They know God's "sorrow" for those who are indifferent toward or rejecting of God. They are persons living almost exclusively by faith. They do not lose heart or hope. They love with the charity of Christ and share in Christ's agony, as in the garden of Gethsemane where Jesus prayed, "Father, if this cup cannot pass unless I drink of it, your will be done." (Lk 22:42)

We each have a cup that will not pass unless we drink it. We each have a wine that will make us holy if we drink it. It differs from every other person's cup and drink. Within the personal solitude of sanctification is a tenderly intimate call from God to fidelity and humility, like a pearl dropped into an ocean for which we are to plunge into the depths to receive this treasure from God. Each one is summoned to allow God to fashion a new creation from all the primal gifts we possess—and even from the "mess" we may have made of our lives. From gifts to debris, God will work a tapestry of unique beauty.

The transformation process is a journey to holiness by way of refinement by fire. It is purification by love of all that is not God. This process transforms the poor in spirit to the rich in the kingdom of God. It transforms the child of God by baptism to the spiritual child of God through the cross and suffering, in the likeness of the beloved Son, Jesus Christ. Holiness is to let Christ live his own life fully in us, uniquely nuanced by who we are and not by some other person's gift. We are made holy as God is holy. It is the mystical life at its best.

What Is

I recall it said, "There is nothing perfect on earth. There is only life." There is only life—as though one would say, "It just is!" Judgments are suspended on whether it is satisfying to me or not. "It just is," is life as it happens, to be seen and accepted. The sky is blue today, with a few cumulus clouds floating by. Birds are chirping their specific sounds. Trees are swaying in the gentle breeze. My hand is hurting. My thoughts are rambling, skirting from this to that and over there. "It just is!" Obviously there are causes, but I need to work with what is, regardless of the cause.

There is a time to let things be just as they are, without manipulating what is, or denying any of it. To "let it be," may allow us to see some things as they are for the first time. In the spiritual life, this step of "letting it be as is" cannot be bypassed or dismissed as unnecessarily elemental. Nor does it excuse us of working to make a better world. Looking and pondering, seeing and absorbing, letting "what is" touch us and leave its impact, is sometimes excluded from our prayer life. Yet this is the core of contemplative prayer: receiving. It is what solitude teaches. "What is" has something to give us if we can wait patiently and let it reach us, if we can welcome the meaning of what is as our mentor, if we are willing to be an intimate part of "what is" here and now. "What is" is the gift of life. That life, in its fullness, is eternal life, a life that never ends. To this we have been called by God's mercy, fashioning us from grace to grace into the likeness of Christ Jesus, in greater and more complete holiness.

Human Choice

Having said the above, I am also keenly aware of the tremendous responsibility we have for our choices and the insidious power of evil in the world. Within the mystery of human life, what we choose has enormous consequences with far-reaching repercussions in our world. We use our free will to harm life or to nurture it, to make decisions for growth and progress or for decline and demise. There is the paradox of good choices and the paradox of sinful choices, choices for life and choices for death. We are free to choose and free to refuse.

Choices that have caused harm to others open us to another mystery: forgiveness and reconciliation. Human choices for death arise from life perceived as "too much at one time." So we choose a respite, anything that might relieve or dissipate the burden we presently bear. We do not choose death as such, but as relief as we perceive it from life's pressured demands. Death follows upon choices that defy life's truth in favor of death's consequences, even while the choice for truth always strives to erupt from our human consciousness to pierce the light of day, to bring us to new freedom.

Human life must one day include the fullness of life. From our deepest core comes an insatiable thirst for completion. When we choose death temporarily and repent, God forgives, God restores. God is always calling us beyond our limits. God waits patiently to give us the fullness of life, the completion of which will be known in eternity. Human life is called to deification; we are called to share in divine life, because God wants our full participation in the mystery of love. Fullness of human life is the transformation of the person by love into Christ, whose dying and rising has sealed for us the eternal glory that waits for us in the kingdom of God. "Your reign of love come; Your will be done, O gracious and merciful God. You alone are our fullness. You alone, our complete bliss!"

That All May Be One

As Christ lives in us more fully, we are bonded more strongly to others. The mystery of solitude reaches everyone and unites with every human emotion and experience. Within the ravages of human struggle and pain, a communion erupts where every person incorporated in Christ Jesus is my mother and my brother and my sister.

Solitude cradles the spirituality of communion and rocks to sleep the divisions among peoples that create a culture of death. Solitude is clearly a culture of life and, therefore, an ambience of communion. Life is shared in solitude, cherished unto dying for it—the real life of unbroken spiritual solidarity. "Death is at work in us," so that life in one body and one spirit rises slowly, surely, from the ashes of a flaming fire. In solitude one cannot forget the needs of others anymore than one can cease praying, without belying the purpose of solitude. Within solitude one tastes, by faith, the deepest spirit of communion in the profound *gift of compassion*.

Through, with, and in Christ Jesus, we are both alone and in communion with everyone. We are also never alone again, as long as there is a person who is suffering, helpless, weak, and sinful—from these none are excluded. The gift of compassion bursts through every cloud of resistance as it patiently, tenderly, walks the common line of human suffering, shared and endured together. Compassion has the uncanny power to lift and carry away every division among peoples by the sheer gift of love and communion. Compassion enables us to endure in love all the sufferings human beings undergo and, therefore, unites all persons in an inseparable bond of communion.

"The glory that you [Father] have given me I have given them, so that they may be one, as we are one, I in them and you in me, that they may be completely one, so that the world may know that you have sent me and have loved them even as you have loved me" (Jn 17:22–23). In this magnificent revelation by Jesus in his last discourse, he opens his Heart in a profound prayer, to spill the promise that we are already in deepest communion with God and with one another through the efficacy of Jesus' divine plea. In him we live and move and have our being, together.

Solitude That Kills

The most terrible negative solitude is sin: alienation from God, alienation from others, alienation from oneself. We become estranged from the most beautiful solitude we are created to be, a solitude for God, a garden enclosed to receive deity. God wants our divinization, and we say no by sinning. It is more desecrating than destroying the canvas of a splendid master-piece of art because one cannot tolerate the inevitable human error or imperfection in some part of it. In sinning, we never fully accept the human condition as it is, but try to deny it rather than learn from it the obedience, surrender, and self-giving we owe our Creator and Lord. The deliberate estrange-ment and rejection of God—chosen when we sin, fully and freely—is a rupture in the communion in love that God has established and wants for each of us for all eternity. Will we kill this life? Will we remain in the solitude of death?

Only one human being has endured the full brunt of human solitude. Only one human person of divine origin could assume the solitude of sin in all its ramifications with-out being ultimately destroyed by it. Jesus Christ transformed that solitude of death into a solitude of life. "But thanks be to God who gives us the victory through our Lord Jesus Christ." (I Cor 15:57)

Everyone, My Brother and Sister

Everyone in any given community is a solitude to another, for no one fully understands or fully identifies with another; nevertheless, each solitude is in communion with others, as everyone is bonded and joined in Christ. The transformation God effects in me, affects you. Your transformation in Christ

redounds to me. Link-by-link, our human destinies inter-
twine, and there is no going to God alone. God purifies and
transforms each member within the solitude that she or he is,
tailoring the purification/transformation process to suit each
one's needs toward becoming holy. But that transpires within
the larger horizon of human solidarity and communion. The
communion may not be recognized or even desired; however,
it is the way of God, the way modeled by the triune life in
God. The Spirit of God accomplishes, in each unique solitude
of every person, the hollowing and hallowing necessary for
union with Christ in love and union with each other in Christ.
Therefore, the spirituality of solitude can be considered a spirituality of communion—and the spirituality of communion, a
spirituality of solitude. How can one ever be alone? How can
one ever live in communion without encountering solitude?

The wondrous mystery is that God wants the solitude and
the communion of a lover, a nuptial union, with each person.
Each one is beloved; each called to intimacy with God, the
beloved. Each single member is joined with every other member; each member is called to be one with the other in Christ.
Were we to fully live the spirituality of communion, we might
discover that spears have been pounded into ploughshares,
that we might work together rather than war against each
other. "They will not hurt or destroy on all my [God's] holy
mountain." (Isa 11:9)

We can hope for the day when divisions will gradually
diminish and, eventually, vanish if we ascribe to a spirituality
of communion. Then the culture of life will thrive on earth,
in those who choose it. One day it will lead us into eternity,
where our communion with all those who have passed to God

and glory will participate in the never-ending sharing of life and love, in the great solitude of one God in three Persons. Everyone, one with God. Everyone, one with each other. Oh, God, accomplish what you desire! "When, joined, they would rejoice

> In eternal song;
> For He was the Head
> Of this bride of His
>
> To whom all the members
> Of the just would be joined,
> Who form the body of the bride.
> He would take her
>
> Tenderly in His arms
> And there give her His love;
> And when they were thus one,
> He would lift her to the Father"[3]

Chapter 10

The Cross of Solitude

It fills me with hesitancy and trepidation to speak of the cross of solitude which, cannot be presented glibly or irreverently without losing its profound meaning. A cross contains a blessing and a blitzing, a saving grace and a tempting scandal. It can never be sentimentalized, lest it be denied for what it must truly be: a contradiction. Yet contradictions carry the stark two sides of one reality. What we believe to be contradictory, may, in God's eyes, be more consonant and, therefore, more necessary than we can see at first sight.

Can being in solitude with God really be a cross? A deeper question: can we, as weak, limited, sinful persons truly be one with God, so that there are no contradictions? No crossing of our wills with God's in disagreement or resistance? Since we cannot admit the latter, a cross will always stretch across our path when we are in solitude with God.

In solitude, one must be willing to taste his or her own inner poverty, to have the courage to feel God touch the sensitivities we have as human beings—limited, weak, and sinful—and to know our propensity to spurn God in foolish arrogance. Solitude belies any evasion of reality and, if we are true to it, solitude will spew before our eyes the hypocrisy by which we live. As a true friend, solitude will remind us that the love we have received from God is not earned or deserved. Therefore, our receptivity to this saving love must be an act of humility, which renders to God praise and thanksgiving for the gift.

Solitude will fashion us in true humility by reason of the naked absence of gratification for our proud egos. We must be willing to be exposed. Solitude will ask us to yield to the will of One who knows what is best for us. We are no longer number one on center stage. The dethroned ego has yielded to divine truth. Henceforth, the only way forward is into greater truth, no matter what the cost.

Solitude ignores our myopic rationalizations that we are our own masters with sufficient power to effect our sanctification or, at least, to do enough to merit a great reward. Utter foolishness! A cross is often of our own making! Part of the experience of solitude is to unmask for us the cross of our own making, as well as the cross that arises from circumstances and situations beyond our control. More painfully, solitude reveals the cross that comes from God to his trusted friends who share Jesus' passion and death before resurrection comes.

All of our experiences in sharing the mystery of the cross are forms of suffering, deep ones. All of our experiences can transform us, sooner or later, if we accept, through faith, the workings of the Holy Spirit, who fashions us into the likeness of Jesus Christ. What is certain is that our cross of purification or reparation it will be delicately tuned to our personality, gifts, weaknesses, and sins. It will suit us "just fine." The uniqueness of our own tailored cross makes it a personal solitude experience, unknown fully to anyone else. Yet the commonality of suffering, pain, and self-emptying makes the cross an experience of spiritual communion with everyone. Again, love is the meaning. Suffering borne in love is the bonding between persons. Love effects this communion with

God, with ourselves, and with everyone in the human race. It is what brings true freedom, casting out fear.

The Cross and Liberation

So how does the cross shape our liberation? What share in the life of the Crucified will be ours to fill up the sufferings of Christ? We need to identify the cruciform ways solitude can nail us to the wood. A scripture quote that has nourished my spiritual life for too many years to count comes from St. Paul's Letter to the Galatians 2:19–20: "With Christ I am nailed to the Cross and I live, now no longer I, but Christ lives in me."

Over several years, I have discovered my understanding of these words have changed many times, adding new insights to its meaning. It is one of similar scripture passages that carry contradictions unable to be penetrated except through faith and the personal experience of one's share in Christ's sufferings.

"Nailed" to death, and yet I live. I live, but no—Christ lives in me. I seek liberation and I am riveted. There is freedom in the outstretched arms of our Savior, pinned to the tree. Strange as these contradictions seem, they are, of necessity, the light and the dark of the spiritual life, the sacrifice that gains the victory, the love that pays every debt, the way of Calvary that leads to resurrection. If we are to embrace the cross, it must be with the confident faith that God knows and does what is best for us, even in turning the crosses of our own making into ways of saving grace. All things work together for good—and often good we do not see—for those who follow the way of Jesus.

I seek to clarify this by analogy with the moment-to-moment changes in the sun as it spans the sky from sunrise to sunset. The earth's movement positions us to see the sun from different vantage points in the trajectory, as it changes in appearance from the first burst of new glow to the mounting intensity of high noon, to the gradual waning to twilight gleam, and finally, to its loss from our sight.

Our seeking of God is as constant as the sun, this ever-present search, day and night, for that union in love with the God who has called us to share his life and love. In this precious journey of life, marked by its changing circumstances, seeking God takes various forms and undergoes many transformations before our life sets in the West, or better, in the "East"!—another paradox. Solitude is the "divine milieu" that enhances the traveler, much like the environment in which we breathe. Some days, the atmosphere is heavy and humid; other days it is light and clear. Some days the skies hold storm clouds; other days, thunder, lightning, and torrents of rain; some days are bitter cold, with snowfall in abundance; other days, the unbearable oven of a burning heat pervades our life. The cross is in all of these as one endures the solitude of each change in his or her life. *The transformative power of our endurance of the cross in our lives rests upon our correspondence, in self-surrender, to the process of death and dying.* How far we want to go depends on the purification needed, our generosity, and what God wants to effect in us.

At one point solitude itself will be a cross. Stripped of the pleasurable distractions that can dissipate the process of transformation, we must embrace the cross without compromise. There will be days, many perhaps, when solitude will feel less like a heavenly haven and more like the burning sands of utter emptiness, scorching every form of life in us. Some days, we may long for the death that will relieve us from the present burden—or so we may think. At this peak of God's work of transformation in us, when we may want to retreat or abandon the way, God will ask the greatest fidelity. Unknown to us, new life is just around the corner.

If we refuse to compromise or abort the process, gently and perseveringly we can discover that the truth does set us free. The fears we have of the cross are separated from the "fear of fear," and the former become bearable as they are seen as a gift of God enlightening us and liberating us. We are being freed to love as deeply as the laying down of one's life as Jesus did. The sufferings of this process cannot compare, as St. Paul assures us, to the glory prepared for us in eternity.

As Catherine de Heuck Dougherty explains, [The *poustinik*, or the person in solitude] has become so empty that he is simply one who carries God.[1] Kenosis or self-emptying is required for the fullness of divine life to "birth and bloom" after the seed has fallen into the ground and died. Resurrection always follows a cross borne in love. One created anew now has the heart and spirit of Christ Jesus. "No longer I, but Christ lives in me." This is no light platitude. It is a profound mystery of pure faith. But, oh, the pain! It is as one who "goes into hell alive," as was mentioned previously. St. John of the Cross explains: "For this purgation is that which would have to be undergone there. The soul that endures it here on earth either does not enter purgatory or is detained there for only a short while. It gains more in one hour here on earth by this purgation than it would in many there."[2] "Hail, Cross, our only hope!" From the contradiction of the cross in our lives, a vertical beam always reaches toward heaven and final glory.

Chapter 11

A Solitude Mystery:
The Transfiguration, Jesus' and Ours

For many years, I have pondered in awe and bewilderment the astonishing revelation of the mystery of Jesus' transfiguration on Mount Tabor. The place may be contended, the happening disputed or denied; nonetheless, the mystery of the transformation of our bodies and spirits in the likeness of Jesus' resurrection, anticipated by Tabor's transfiguration, is trustworthy of our belief and honored by our exploration.

The account of Jesus' transfiguration by all three synoptic writers leaves no doubt of its significance. Peter later uses that experience as a credential to his apostolic witness of Jesus Christ: "But we had been eyewitnesses of his majesty. For he received honor and glory from God the Father, when that voice was conveyed to him by the Majestic Glory, saying 'This is my Son, my Beloved with whom I am well pleased.' We ourselves heard this voice come from heaven, while we were with him on the holy mountain." (2 Pet 1:16–18)

When an incident has been recorded in the scriptures three times for posterity, and reference made to it elsewhere, we do well to stand alert and listen. There is a marvel here that needs to be heard many times and prayed with even more times. My personal attraction to this event, besides the feast being the day of my own baptism (a great privilege and grace), rests more deeply in a *solitude of wonder* before God's twofold revelation of glory:

1. the manifestation of Jesus' changed appearance—brilliant, shining as the sun, with clothes turned dazzling white—as a presage of resurrection; and

2. the proclamation of the voice from heaven: "This is my Son, the Beloved; he enjoys my favor. Listen to him." (Lk 9:35)

A Solitude of Wonder: Changed Appearance

I am in wonder at the beauty of such a transfigured face that radiates God's blinding light and is tempered to us, as human beings, much like the face of Moses when God spoke to him. Moses had to cover his face, so that the brilliance would not harm the people. "The skin on his face was radiant that they could not venture near him." (Ex 34:29–30)

What transfigures in glory the splendid beauty of a human face? Whence comes the transformation? *It is the light from within*. At the transfiguration, the Father released in Jesus the divine splendor within, beauty like no other, the very glory of God, so that, through the words of the apostles, we might glimpse it for a fleeting moment.

Were one to look upon the brilliant face of Jesus, would one not recoil, shield his or her eyes, as if turned toward the burning sun? Such dazzling brightness would burn our tender receptors. God dared to unveil his inner radiance, for a brief moment, to fill with joy those he loved and to fortify them for suffering. The Father, in loving mercy, enabled the three apostles to look upon the transfigured body of Christ, so that the experience, never forgotten, would assure them of Jesus' ultimate victory when the resurrection occurred. With Jesus' resurrection and ours, we hope for the day when there will be no need to shield our eyes before God. With eyes unveiled, we shall behold him in glory.

In my wonder, I also experience the mystery of solitude: "I cannot see God and live," in this earthly inhabitance. I cannot tolerate, in my mortal body, the vision of God. The solitude of wonder carries both an invitation to draw near, to be in God's presence when God reveals himself, and a promise that one day we shall be "clothed over," transfigured so as to behold God in glory. St. Paul has assured us, "When Christ who is your life is revealed, then you also will be revealed with him in glory." (Col 3:4)

The solitude of wonder means I stand alone before God in watchful waiting. I stand with expectation and trust. Waiting, I believe the promise will reach completion. In wonder, I hope for the fulfillment that leads to communion with God and with the saints in eternal life.

Voice From Heaven

Regarding the voice of the Father saying, "This is my Son, my Beloved; he enjoys my favor," how does one respond before this wonder except in the silent solitude of awe and receptivity? The Father has spoken. We are hearing from God the marvelous expression of his utter delight in the beloved Son. Jesus, the chosen one, receives the complete and joyous favor of the Father, who is totally satisfied with Jesus' fulfillment of all the Father wills. We are privy to this awesome intimacy in the words spoken. "This is my Son." John of the Cross knew this wonder when he said, "The Father spoke one Word, which was His son, and this word He always speaks in eternal silence, and in silence must It be heard by the soul."[1]

Jesus who "enjoyed God's favor" was transfigured and seen by Peter, James, and John for their and our encouragement. This event followed the prediction of the passion and death of Jesus, which would be enough to shake the ground beneath the faith of the disciples unless they tasted a portion of the promise of resurrection. How tenderly the Father opened his heart to reveal what would be the culmination of the passion when the victory would be won and death conquered! In this glory, let loose for a moment, hope was born, because in Jesus would be fulfilled all that the Father desires for us. The Father was utterly happy with the total self-giving of Jesus! Jesus "was happy. The Transfiguration is a mystery of divine happiness. The whole stream of joy that flows between the Father and Son, which is the Holy Spirit himself, 'overflowed' the vessel of Christ's humanity on this occasion."[2]

Then, lest we forget or remain dumbfounded, the Father commanded us gently, "listen to Him." Here is a tender, intimate command of the Father revealing the way to him: my beloved Son holds every word you must hear to be one with me.

We see, in this gospel passage, the wonder of the Father's intimacy with the Son. We see the Son's acceptance in his humanity of the Father's radiance and splendor. We see the profound humility of Father and Son to open to the apostles and to us, in turn, a peek into glory that could only be seen in the Spirit of love. The solitude of wonder touches the extreme poverty that is ours, so we may understand such revelation without stammering, like Peter, to build three tents of irrelevance! Human solitude! Before such splendor we are left with nothing to do but give thanks and praise. That is our privileged human destiny. It is the call of the contemplative life in the church. In wonder, our sacred solitude opens us to participate in divine splendor through the gift of love inviting us into glory.

The Father's voice was "from the cloud," which came to overshadow the apostles. The cloud and overshadowing have immense symbolic meaning, and refer to the account in Exodus, of the theophany to Moses on Mt. Sinai, and in I Kings 19, to Elijah on Mt. Horeb—as both Moses and Elijah were conversing with Jesus at the transfiguration—as well as to the Annunciation of the Virgin Mary, to the Ascension, and to every mystical experience in which God effects an all-powerful deed, baffling our clouded understanding. "The cloud in the Transfiguration, then, becomes what the dove is at baptism: the visible sign of the presence of the Holy Spirit. Besides, how could the Spirit be absent in a theophany that is so clearly Trinitarian? . . . The very light that radiates from Christ is none other than the Holy Spirit, who was dwelling in his flesh."[3] The cloud symbolically also suggests the ambience of solitude, when God comes to those who are alone, either physically or circumstantially.

It is as though God, whose works are often secret and hidden, needs to hide from us the immensity of his power, so as not to frighten us into resistance. We would, like the apostles, "fall on our faces, overcome with fear." We need clouds to shield us from the immensity of God. These very clouds also, paradoxically, offer us a temporary excuse, in our human poverty, when we do not respond fully to God, when we fail to live by faith.

God's ways seem "clouded" to our senses, so that our spirits may be overshadowed by the Holy Spirit of God, whose presence is as powerful as a mighty wind and as gentle as a whispered breeze. God seems to ease into solitude our faculties that could impede the overshadowing he wants to effect in us for his own purposes. Then, remain we must in this imposed and necessary solitude, so that the transfiguration process in us is not hindered from accomplishing our total purification and, subsequently, our complete receptivity to God. Whether staying awake or drifting into a mild stupor, as the apostles did, we too can experience the Taboric splendor of God revealed within the center of our souls as we listen to Jesus throughout our Christian lives. Receptive to the Spirit's enlightenment, perhaps—as did Peter, James, and John—on Mt. Tabor—we may turn and see only Jesus. "What can bring us happiness, many say. Let the light of your face shine on us, O Lord." (Ps 4:6)

Though we may want to stay on the Mount, there is a time to come down from Tabor—and to speak of it to no one, for who could understand? Transfigured, we may hope that our lives will reveal "only Jesus."

Chapter Twelve

With God, All Things Are Possible

Does enduring what has been described in previous chapters seem impossible? Most surely, by human standards and ability. It is utterly impossible for any human being to conceive of or to undergo the process of transformation, but by the grace of God. However, we are not in the realm of human accomplishment; we are not in a process of human instigation or fabrication. Solitude and its workings are only undertaken from God, in God, and toward God. With God, all things are possible. The possibility of union with God in love is what God wants to realize in each of us. Who are we to doubt his will or question his gifts? God wants our complete happiness in him.

When one says "yes" to God, "let it be," there is an avalanche of consequences, unforeseen, and not foreknown. God has a divine orchestration in our lives, and God intends a new song to flow from a new creation, over many years of self-giving and many trials of suffering. So when I choose to live for God, I choose also the consequences as they emerge, one by one, on the journey. As the Blessed Virgin's consent to God's message through the angel Gabriel was a moment of "yes" to God's will, and became an endless "be it done to me," it carried, as every commitment does, a lifetime of consequences, even to the death of her son and God on the heights of Calvary. This commitment requires a fiat, repeated and strengthened at every point of the journey. "Yes" must be our constant utterance to whatever God asks of us. Mary, the Mother of God, "heard the Word who does not shout in the streets, because she abided in the silence and expectation where alone the Word is to be heard."[1] Each new surrender of ourselves to God opens our capacity for more self-giving. Saying it once when we make commitments is not enough. Every day brings a new opportunity and a challenge to renew and strengthen that commitment. "Do with me what you will, Lord" is a constant mantra because it affirms consent to God's Spirit in whatever is asked of us. Fidelity in our commitments is what God desires of us.

Commitment

In our day, we hear many who defy the making of permanent commitments. They argue, "How can I commit myself permanently to something when things change? I need to keep open to new options." Or, as the saying goes, "Can anyone say forever?" Can commitments remain unbroken in our day? Perhaps you have heard others say, "If the person I marry becomes, after fifteen years, someone different than I have known, how can I remain committed to her or him?" Or, "Commitment is a relative matter; it is only for a specific time when I knew the circumstances." How clever can be the rationalizations! How untrue to love and its demands!

We readily acknowledge the seeming "impossibility" of dealing with terrible consequences when a beloved husband is killed in military service, leaving a wife and children with little financial support. We have seen the devastating aftermath of a prominent, strong, promising athlete who becomes a paraplegic from a spinal injury. We see countless unforeseen tragedies that wipe away all enthusiasm for living and fill us with a keen awareness of the inability, humanly, to deal with these horrendous happenings. Unless one turns to God, it all remains impossible to endure.

One could not endure without faith and grace. I suggest considering a new viewing point. It can be called "the view from within the theological virtues." If we are living a deeply pervasive faith life, if we are constantly relying upon God in hope, if we pray unceasingly from the love of God that is poured into us, we will see without doubt that with our God nothing is impossible to endure. The human suffering, sorrow, and agony does not necessarily diminish—it is real and cannot be dismissed. But we will be able to recognize that the most devastating tragedy holds an invitation to surrender our plans, destiny, and future goals more completely to God, in what is, here and now, a reality in our lives. It may require an effort beyond our abilities—and that is precisely true. God gives beyond our abilities; God sustains our efforts to believe; God will be the end of our pursuit. This theological viewpoint beholds, from within God, a wisdom and providence only God can impart to us.

In time we will gain new vision, perhaps much later, to understand the moment of tragedy as a blessing in disguise, as we saw in John of the Cross, who, during his Toledo imprisonment, gave birth to the loveliest of bridal poems, the fruit of the spiritual marriage God had effected in him in his darkest moment. God builds on ruins and so do the saints.

Who can explain what happens when those whose lives are lived entirely for God and in God are plunged into a test of faith beyond imagining? In our darkest moments, it may seem that God is no longer supporting us, no longer "real." Where does one turn? To whom shall we go? "With God, all things are possible." But where is God? The cry of anguish screams to the heavens.

Believing Without Seeing

This cry has met the lips of countless persons: those who seldom pray, as well as those who spend many hours in solitary communion with God. Where is the "You" I am seeking so eagerly? Deep within the caverns of mystical union is a gem of faith. It is a gift of believing beyond seeing, a gift that takes us directly to God and into God's mystery. This faith is built upon no surer foundation than God alone. It is a faith that relies upon the Word of God and draws all its strength from God's promises and steadfast love. God is faithful. God cannot deny himself. With God, all things are possible. But can we wait? Can we trust? Are we able to surrender all human securities to rely upon the living and merciful God whose ways are true? Are we willing to leap off the cliff, trusting God will sustain us in our fall?

The saints are those fools for Christ who leap. They are solitude's humble children, whose simple, constant life of union with God changes the world for the better. Like quiet yeast, they activate the spirit of love, kindness, and compassion, unobtrusively, with a constant trust in God that relies upon the steadfast mercy of One who loves us. They are those who have passed from death into life, even on this earth. They are those who know the solitude of holiness and have paid the price. They have lost their lives to passing realities, so as to gain their true life in God forever. "Very truly I tell you, unless a grain of wheat falls into the earth and dies, it remains just a simple grain; but if it dies, it bears much fruit." (Jn 12:24)

No mountain is insurmountable with God. Some mountains God may not want us to surmount, but to circumvent. There is no happening, however tragic, that cannot be met with the gift of God's love. Each experience of hell and death contains, in embryo, the opening to new life. But the mountains, the tragic experiences, the hell-like death, do not necessarily evolve in the manner we desire or decide. Some tragedies seem to remain so for many years, without break in their sorrow or loss. Perhaps it is because God knows we need to remain so for other purposes. Within the tragedy is a message from God, a call to surrender to the mercy and love of One whose ways of wisdom and compassion exceed our frail understanding. Ours is to enter into the flow of divine grace and love that transforms, however painfully, every human tragedy. "If you find your delight in the Lord, he will grant your heart's desire." (Ps 8:17)

Love's Beauty

When "perfect union of love between God and the soul is wrought, she desires to employ herself in those things proper to love. . . . First, she desires to receive the joy and savor of love . . . 'Let us rejoice, Beloved.' Second, she desires to become like the Beloved . . . 'And let us go forth to behold ourselves in your beauty.' Third, she desires to look closely at and know the things and secrets of the Beloved himself . . . 'And further, deep into the thicket.' "[2]

I have never read, apart from the gospels, a more magnificent expounding of that union with God in love than that expressed by St. John of the Cross in *The Spiritual Canticle*, as seen through the attribute of God's beauty. It is a splendid passage of what God effects in the whole person who cherishes God's gift and welcomes it. The beloved of God speaks: "'And let us go forth to behold ourselves in your beauty,' This means: Let us so act that by means of this loving activity we may attain to the vision of ourselves in your beauty in eternal life. That is: That I be so transformed in your beauty that we may be alike in beauty, and both behold ourselves in your beauty, possessing now your very beauty; this, in such a way that each looking at the other may see in the other his own beauty, since both are your beauty alone, I being absorbed in your beauty; hence, I shall see you in your beauty and you shall see me in your beauty, and I shall see myself in you in your beauty, and you will see yourself in me in your beauty; that I may resemble you in your beauty, and you resemble me in your beauty, and my beauty be your beauty and your beauty my beauty; wherefore, I shall be you in your beauty and you will be me in your beauty because your very beauty will be my beauty; and therefore, we shall behold each other in your beauty."[3]

To read this is enough to make one utterly dumbfounded with its incomprehensibility. It is not a matter of the head but of the heart. How does one dare to conceive of this union as possible? We do not conceive it; God has and has willed it to be so. Ours is to receive the gift after espousing the process of purification and self-giving in all its ramifications in our personal lives. We are asked to receive this astonishing gift of God, which is ours for the asking and for the dying. "O the depths of the riches and wisdom and the knowledge of God!

How unsearchable are his judgments and how inscrutable his ways!" (Rom 11:33)

When God chooses to bring us to that "beholding each other in your beauty," we shall have been given an "awakening" in which "the soul feels a strange delight in the breathing of the Holy Spirit in God, in which it is sovereignly glorified and taken with love. . . . It is a spiration that God produces in the soul, in which . . . he breathes the Holy Spirit in it . . . rousing its love with divine excellence and delicacy according to what it beholds in him. Since the breathing is filled with good and glory, the Holy Spirit, through this breathing, filled the soul with good and glory in which he enkindled it in love of himself, indescribably and incomprehensibly, in the depths of God."[4]

This teaching is that of St. John of the Cross, a Carmelite doctor of the universal church, who himself was gifted with this spiritual marriage with God in his lifetime. Although this gift is rare on earth, it presages the union God wants for all of us after this earthly life. Before such a gift and grace from God, we human persons bow in humble expectation and gratitude and surrender to the overwhelming workings of God who has made us "little less than a god." (Ps 8:5)

The blessing of being human is the invitation to participate in God's benevolent design in calling us to an intimate union with the Trinity and fullness of life and bliss in glory one day. Yet we also know our iniquity is as great as to crucify the Son of God. Oh, but for the grace of God! In earthen vessels, we carry the gift of solitude that can welcome God and respond in loving surrender.

"O my Three, my All, my Beatitude, infinite Solitude, Immensity in which I lose myself, I yield myself up to Thee as a prey, bury Thyself in me, that I may bury myself in Thee, while awaiting the time to go and contemplate in Thy light the abyss of Thy greatness. Amen."[5] It was Blessed Elizabeth of the Trinity, a Carmelite of Dijon, who prayed these words prior to her death from Addison's disease, which would take her from this world when she was twenty-six years old.

Epilogue

The prayer of praise abounds in the hearts of those who bow before the lavish self-gift of God to all people. "Praise the Lord, all you nations! Extol him, all you peoples!" (Ps 117:1)

"This praise [that each of the blessed in his own degree of glory gives continually to God] is like the beauty of music. Each one possesses God's gifts differently, each one sings His praise differently, and all of us together form a symphony of love, as of music."[1] These words of St. John of the Cross tell of the beauty revealed in the gifts God has given to each person and the spiritual communion that exists, one to another. Within each life, solitude has had a place. It resonates with the whole of life, similar to the chamber hall of a large symphony orchestra of various instruments whose performers strive for delicate harmony.

In the first chapter of this book, I spoke of the aspects of silence. If we use the analogy of a symphony, this silencing, silenced, and silent solitude can be likened to the delicate expression of rests between long scores of composition. We can liken the composition to our journey of faith. Without the pauses of some instruments while others carry the melody, there would be a cacophony. The discipline of restraint and timing requires a silencing for the sake of beauty and harmony. So it is that silence in solitude enables the beauty of restfulness to be appreciated, the expansiveness of diversity to be honored, the balance of differences to be reverenced, the "sounds" of love to be heard in our lives.

In Chapter Two, "Presence and 'Absence': Felt or Believed," the theme is similar to the changes in tempo between the many modes of a concerto with its andante, adagio, and allegro tempos. These are the variances in the spiritual life that move us to experience the flux of playful courtship between God and the person. We need to experience the contrasts in our lives, in order that we may learn from each change, each experience.

Chapter Three, where we saw idols shatter and demons emerge, portrays the struggle between light and darkness, good and evil, dissonance and harmony in the spiritual journey, as also in a symphony. Tensions bring intensification; boundaries favor creativity; struggles encourage a confrontation, which strives for concord and resolution. As this music fills the chamber of solitude with sometimes tragic sounds resolved only after scores of discordant experiences, we need to listen more carefully and endure the dissonance. These confrontations bring us wisdom and inner strength, a deeper intimacy, and a more profound integrity.

In Chapter Four, "Solitude's Intimacy," we began to see the musical composition expand into a larger theme, a crescendo of deep love that swirls throughout the entire composition. Like music, solitude is "heard" as the voice of the beloved whispering tender manifestations of desire for union. The precious fruit of solitude is love enlarging in endless swellings to become the air one breathes, in order to live.

Prayer, as in Chapter Five, leads to "Solitude's Savorings" in Chapter Six, which are likened to the profound enjoyment of music resounding within the spirit of each listener. The spirit expands, is set free to relish the beauty, to breathe in the loveliness, to abound in delight. God is "known," in the depth of the solitude experience, as the giver of music within the soul. God is tasted as the supreme good ravishing the soul with love, as does great music to the spirit of one who imbibes the beauty of artistry. Listening becomes the abiding disposition that the person in solitude consistently nourishes; listening is an endless waiting on God for God's word and his will to be made manifest.

Within every joy is a sorrow. "Solitude's Sufferings" (Chapter Seven) and cross (Chapter Ten) form the tragedy stirring in every great musical composition, which swirls the intensity of reality through heights of pain and anguish. The music soars. The contrasts press for prominence. The self-giving of the solitary person grows clear, generous, and sonorous. Love is the meaning for solitude to emerge into "The Spirituality of Communion," as we saw in Chapters Eight and Nine. The music encompasses everyone exposed to it as solitude envelops everyone who enters it, only to extend the person outward to embrace every human in one's life of prayer. There is a repeated cycle of entering within and being expelled outward, union with God and service to others. The music repeats.

Shall we not say all things are possible (Chapter Eleven) when God wants the human person to come to complete union with the Trinity in love? Most surely this union can be hoped for, if the person embraces all that God wants to do in her life to accomplish that union. We are created for such intimacy. We are not only conditioned for it but also immersed, in our deepest longings, within the mystery of self-giving love. Intimacy is both the composition and the finale in the concerto of God's desire for us.

Music has a soul, "a symphony of spiritual music" as John of the Cross said earlier; it reverberates throughout every movement of the entire composition. This is God's life in the person. From the depths of prayer in solitude, our soul, filled with God's Spirit, sings forth the love that reverberates in the core of our being as gift and is released to the hearts of all people. John of the Cross writes, "Ecstasy is nothing else than going out of self and being caught up in God."[2] So it is: once caught up in God and sharing God's life of love, the person radiates to others the wonder of God's exquisite beauty and goodness. The love of God is able to go forth unhampered by the ego interests, which were so prevalent before this transformation of the soul took place. Free to give, the person enriches the lives of others. A new spirit and a new soul have been born from the womb of solitude.

As loving prayer flowing out of solitude perdures and pervades, ascends and accelerates, expands and enlarges, it has no boundaries. It diffuses to the hearts of all people and to the throne of God. It becomes a cycle of unending communication from God to human persons and all creation, and back to God, to be caught up into trinitarian life. "Those who love me I also love, and those who seek me find me" (Prov 8:17). More and more we share in the circle of love between Father, Son, and Holy Spirit. The solitude of God within the community of God is one. The solitude of human persons within the community of God becomes one. "I in you and you in me," says the Lord. A new song bursts forth now into all creation. Music fills the heavens, and we are caught up in the eternal song of praise to God. With God, all things are possible. All honor, glory, and praise be to you, O God, now and forever! *Let the solitude sound!*

Desire

Desire, unceasing desire for God, will be with those who pray, until solitude has done its work of transformation in Christ. God will capture the hearts of people, leaving them so touched by love that they have no desire other than to belong to God by consent, as they belong to God by creation and grace. We are destined to be transformed in Christ by love.

This *desire* was not our human initiative. God first desires us. Fr. William A. Barry, SJ, when speaking of the God who seeks us, says: "God's desire creates what God finds desirable. God's desire for us makes us, and makes us desirable to God. We exist only because of God's desire, and we will exist forever, as the object of God's desire. God is always seeking us."[3]

For some people, solitude is a preparation for mission, as with the prophet, Elijah, St. John the Baptist, St. Paul the Apostle, and Jesus himself. For others, solitude is itself the mission, as in the lives of St. Anthony the hermit, Bl. Paul Guistiniani, or the Carthusians. The Carmelite tradition of prayer in solitude has flourished in the church through saints, such as Teresa of Jesus, John of the Cross, Thèrése of Lisieux, Teresa Benedicta (Edith Stein), and many others not yet canonized. Holy men and women have also known the sanctifying effect of solitude from within the midst of intense service to others, as in the life of Blessed Teresa of Calcutta. Still others, after many years of service, suffering, illness, or loss, have known the solitude of diminishment, poverty, and solidarity with those they serve, as did St. Damien of Molokai. Persons, such as Helen Keller, who have lived the major part of their disabled lives receiving service from others, have also known the purifying transformation in solitude by humble acceptance of their situation and by a deep faith life. However and whenever the will of God invites a person into the solitude of transformative love, growth in holiness and union with God will enrich the person's mission in the church.

What astounding mercy our divine beloved lavishes excessively upon all those who seek God—and also on those who do not! Who can seek and not find? Need we fear falling into the hands of the living God, as awesome as it is? All will be lost only to be found anew and transformed.

Wherever you are, whoever you are, whatever you do, know that solitude has an undisputed place in your life, willingly or unwillingly. The sounding solitude of everyone's search for the living God, from beginning to end, in response to God's primary and sustaining initiative, resounds ultimately to the glory of God and the perfecthappiness of each one who chooses the way of love. So, I invite you to become, by God's grace, the Christ of solitude. Become the solitude of Christ wherein he lives. Urge God to fashion you into that transformed person in whom the Trinity, indwelling, consummates by love the union God and we desire. Allow God, by your welcoming of the sacred solitude of your personal life, to pierce the stone-cold fears of failure, frustration, and feverish resistance to grace. Yield to the tender sway of the Holy Spirit whose breath blows through your spirit. Let God fulfill all God's desires to bring you to eternal bliss. As Ruth Burrows explained, "All my concern is that God should have what he wants: the chance to be good to me to his heart's content."[4]

Then God will open your wounded heart, as was Jesus', so that floods of blood and water will self-empty to nourish the church and bring forth new progeny, holy children of God. Love, then, will have triumphed.

> "The bride has entered
> The sweet garden of her desire,
> And she rests in delight,
> Laying her neck
> On the gentle arm of her Beloved."[5]

> "And I gave myself to Him,
> Keeping nothing back;
> Then I promised to be His bride."[6]

> "O my God, when will it be
> That I can truly say:
> Now I live because I do not die?"[7]

Prayer of Solitude

> O holy solitude! Ocean of deep mystery! Haven of God!
> You are laden with divine treasures discovered anew with
>   each opening of your wonders.
> You hold silence as a precious friend, in whose company
>   you seduce the beloved's bride, as she listens to her
>   spouse's lure of love.
> O solitude of holy ground, where shoes are shed and bushes
>   burn in flaming fire, though not consumed!
> You invite charity's gift of self and hold the offering in faith's
>   abode to be nourished and fashioned into a new creation.

O solitude of promise, rich with hope that leans upon the
Word of God and brings comfort and warmth to those
who hear and heed with contrite heart.

You anchor in trust those who feel profound sorrow
for sin and failure, and you enable the crushed spirit
to soar again.

O absolute Solitude, who is God! You are the Mystery, the
Love, the Word who has won my surrendered heart for
the praise of your goodness and glory, Father, Son, and
Holy Spirit.

You give your mercy and compassion to all those who come
to you, that every person may sing forever the glory of
your name.

Through the beloved, Jesus Christ, who always pleased
the Father, we claim the victory he has won over sin
and death.

Inflame us, Beloved, with the Spirit's love, so that sharing
this with others we may all abide, one with you, forever
in glory. Amen.

Notes

Introduction

1 SC, Sts. 26–27.
2 Thomas Merton, *Ascent to Truth* (New York, NY: Harcourt, Brace and Co., 1951).
3 Loren Eiseley, *The Night Country*.
4 LF 3:28.
5 Donald Nichols, *Holiness*, p. 128.
6 LF St. 1, no. 13.
7 SC, St. 38, no. 3.
8 II DN 14:1.
9 Kerry Walters, *Soul Wilderness*, (Mahwah: Paulist Press, 2001), p. 3.
10 "A Search For Solitude: Pursuing the Monks True Life," Thomas Merton, *Journals* vol. 3, ed. Lawrence S. Cunningham (San Francisco: Harper Collins, 1996), p. 28.

Chapter 1

1 Hans Urs von Balthasar, *Elizabeth of the Trinity*.
2 SC, St. 35, no. 1.
3 III Asc. 2:21–22.
4 IC 1:2, no. 9.
5 M/C, no. 21.
6 Br. Romeo Bonsaint, SC, PhD, "Silence and Transcendent Presence" *Spiritual Life*, 2004.
7 Asc. 3:3.
8 St. Thèrése, Act of Oblation to Merciful Love.
9 SC, St. 26.
10 SC, St. 14–15, no. 10.

11 *Walk with Jesus: Stations of the Cross* (Maryknoll, NY: Orbis Books, 1990).
12 SC, St. 13–14.

Chapter 2

1 SC, St. 1, no. 7.
2 Ibid., St. 1, no. 9.
3 II Asc. 9:1.
4 SC, St. 11, St. 12, no. 3.
5 Ibid.
6 SC, St. 1, no 12.
7 I DN, St. 3.
8 II Asc. 4:2.
9 SC, St. 1, no. 21.
10 C.S. Lewis, *The Four Loves*, Chapter 6.
11 John Paul II, *The Theology of the Body*, p. 38.
12 SC, St. 7, no. 9.
13 St. Catherine of Sienna, *Dialogue of Divine Providence*.
14 SC, St. 1, no. 2.
15 II Asc. 4:6.
16 Ibid., 4:4.
17 SC, St. 1, no. 21.
18 Asc. 9:1.

Chapter 3

1 IC, St. 1, no. 9.
2 LF, St. 1, no. 21.
3 *Anthology of Famous English and American Poetry* (New York, NY: Random House, Inc.), p. 84.
4 Edith Stein, *Finite and Eternal Being*, pp. 401–402.

Chapter 4

1 Way 26:9, p. 136.
2 Life, Chapter 19, nos. 11–12.

3   LF, St. 1, no. 3.
4   DN, St. 5.
5   I DN, St. 8.
6   SC, St. 36, no. 4.
7   LF, St. 4.
8   Letter of Elizabeth of the Trinity to Mme. De Sourdon, 1902.
9   Complete Works of Elizabeth of the Trinity, p.64.
10 Jennifer Moorcroft, *He Is My Heaven: The Life of Elizabeth of the Trinity*, p. 108.

Chapter 5

1   Counsels to a religious on how to reach perfection, no. 9, p. 664.
2   SC, St. 28, no. 1.
3   II DN, Chapter 6, no. 1.
4   William Johnston, *Letters to Contemplatives*, p. 103.
5   Ibid.
6   Catherine of Siena, *Dialogue on Divine Providence*, p. 167.

Chapter 6

1   SC, St. 27, no. 7.
2   Gary Ferguson, *Shouting At the Sky*, (St. Martin's Press, New York, 1999), p. 243.

Chapter 7

1   SC, St. 36, no. 12.
2   Ibid.
3   SC, St. 36, no. 10.
4   Ibid., no. 13.
5   I Asc. 4:2–3.
6   IC, VI: 4, no. 12.
7   II DN, Chapter 6, no. 5.
8   Ibid., no. 2.
9   II DN 6:6.

10 SC, St. 29, no. 10.

11 Blommestijn, Huls and Waaijman, *The Footprints of Love.*

12 LF, St. 2, no. 28.

13 SC, St. 35, no. 7.

14 SC, St. 35, no. 3.

15 Ibid., no. 4.

16 LF, St. 3, nos. 78–79.

Chapter 8

1 Joanne Mosley, *Edith Stein: Modern Saint and Martyr* (Hidden Spring, Mahwah, NJ), p. 68.

2 II DN 25:4.

3 SCl, St. 12, no. 7.

4 LF, St. 3, no 79, p. 641.

5 LF, St. 3, no. 79.

6 Ibid., St. 3, no. 9.

7 SC, St. 29, no. 2.

Chapter 9

1 Henri Nouwen, *L'Arche in the World*, p. 165.

2 II DN 5:7.

3 Romances 4:14–15.

Chapter 10

1 Catherine de Heuck Dougherty, *Poustinia*, p. 134.

2 II DN 6:6.

Chapter 11

1 Maxims and Counsels, No. 21, p. 675.

2 Raniero Cantalamessa, OFM, *The Mystery of the Transfiguration*, (Servant Books, St. Anthony Messenger Press).

3 Ibid, p. 29.

Chapter 12

1 Erasmo Leiva-Merikakis, *Fire of Mercy of the Word*, Vol. 2, (Ignatius Press).

2 SC, St. 36, no 3. Edits from Catholic Treasury, with credits to ICS Publications.

3 SC, St. 36, no. 10.

4 LF, St. 4, no. 16–17.

5 Elizabeth of the Trinity, *Pledge of Glory*, p. 4.

Epilogue

1 SC, St. 15, no. 26, p. 413.

2 Maxims and Counsels, no. 80.

3 William A. Barry, S.J. "Seeking God: Addiction, Spirituality, and Recovery" (Houston, TX: National Catholic Council on Alcoholism, 59th Annual Convention).

4 Ruth Burrows, *The Essence of Prayer*.

5 SC. St. 27.

6 SC, St. 18.

7 Stanzas of the Soul That Suffers With Longing to See God: St. 8.

The Institute of Carmelite Studies promotes research and publication in the field of Carmelite spirituality. Its members are Discalced Carmelites, part of a Roman Catholic community—friars, nuns, and laity—who are heirs to the teaching and way of life of Teresa of Jesus and John of the Cross, men and women dedicated to contemplation and to ministry in the Church and the world. Information concerning their way of life is available through local diocesan Vocation Offices or from the Vocation Directors' Offices:

1233 S. 45th Street, Milwaukee, WI 53214

1 Fallons Lane 1628 London, ON, Canada N6A 4C1

P.O. Box 3420, San Jose, CA 95156-3420

5151 Marylake Drive, Little Rock, AR 72206